MW00425647

The Best Practices Enterprise™

A Guide to Achieving Sustainable World-Class Performance

The Best Practices Enterprise™

A Guide to Achieving Sustainable World-Class Performance

JAMES M. KERR

Copyright ©2006 by James M. Kerr

ISBN 1-932159-60-6

Printed and bound in the U.S.A. Printed on acid-free paper
10 9 8 7 6 5 4 3 2 1

Library of Congress Cataloging-in-Publication Data

Kerr, James, 1962-
    The best practices enterprise : a guide to achieving sustainable world-class
performance / by James Kerr.
        p. cm.
    Includes index.
    ISBN-13: 978-1-932159-60-8 (hardcover : alk. paper)
    ISBN-10: 1-932159-60-6 (hardcover : alk. paper)
    1. Benchmarking (Management) 2. Organizational effectiveness.
3. Strategic planning. 4. Industrial management. I. Title.
    HD62.15.K467 2006
    658.4'01--dc22   2006001839

Direct all inquiries to J. Ross Publishing, Inc., 5765 N. Andrews Way, Fort Lauderdale, FL 33309.

Phone: (954) 727-9333
Fax: (561) 892-0700
Web: www.jrosspub.com

For Haley

TABLE OF CONTENTS

List of Figures xi
Preface xv
About the Author xix
Acknowledgments xxi
Web Added Value™ xxiii

Chapter 1: The *Best Practices Enterprise*™—A New Vision for a New Era 1
Imagine: *Your Company, Inc.* 2
The *Best Practices Enterprise*™ Philosophy 10
A Recipe for Lasting Success 12

Chapter 2: Best Practices Business Principles 13
A New Agenda for the New Era 13
The Business Principles 15
With That Said 28

Chapter 3: Program-Centric Strategic Planning 31
Why "More of the Same" Will Not Cut It 32
What Is Program-Centric Strategic Planning? 32
Staying Current 33
The Perfect Program 34
Getting Started 37
As an Aside 42
In Closing 44

Appendix A: Sample Opportunities Identification Documents 47

Chapter 4: Resilient IT Architecture Design **59**
What Is Resilient IT Architecture? 60
The Essence of Architectures 61
The RITA Methodology 64
A Six-Step Approach 66
In Closing 75

Appendix B: Sample Resilient IT Architecture Target **77**
Definition Document

Chapter 5: Portfolio-Based Project Management **105**
The Age of Free Agency Is Upon Us 106
Other Obstacles to Consider 107
The Portfolio-Based Project Management Structure 109
Common Hazards 118
Critical Success Factors 119
In Closing 122

Chapter 6: Uninterrupted Business Redesign **123**
Why Bother with Uninterrupted Business Redesign? 124
The Keys to U-BPR 126
How to Make It Stick 134
In Closing 136

Appendix C: Sample Value Chain Case Study **137**

Chapter 7: Results-Focused Communications **141**
A Results-Focused Communications Program 143
Getting Results-Focused Communications Off the Ground 145
Communication Vehicles 147
A Few Pointers 154
In Closing 156

Chapter 8: Cross-Cultural Workforce Inclusion **159**
Defining the Business Case for Cross-Cultural Workforce Inclusion 161
Setting the Program in Motion 162
Maintaining Momentum through Corporate Officer Designation 169
Watch for Roadblocks 171
Winning the Diversity Game 172
In Closing 174

Chapter 9: Continuous Employee Improvement **175**
The Continuous Employee Improvement Continuum 177
CEI Strategy Planning 179
Driving the CEI Program 186
In Closing 192

Postscript: Final Thoughts **193**
What Sets *Best Practices Enterprises*™ Apart? 193
Time to Get Going 195

Appendix D: Sample Continuous Employee Improvement **197**
Project Baseline Report

Index **211**

LIST OF FIGURES

Chapter 1

Figure 1.1. Fitting all the best practices together is our challenge.

Chapter 2

Figure 2.1. The business principles form a solid foundation for the best practices.

Chapter 3

Figure 3.1. Strategic planning is the first piece of the puzzle.
Figure 3.2. A simplified program-centric strategic planning framework.

Chapter 4

Figure 4.1. IT architecture is the next practice to add.
Figure 4.2. An analogy for understanding IT architecture.
Figure 4.3. Work begins with a baseline assessment of the individual elements of the IT environment before an integrated RITA can be defined.
Figure 4.4. The four dimensions of a RITA plan.
Figure 4.5. Sample baseline template excerpt.
Figure 4.6. The RITA methodology's continuous process improvement loop.

Appendix B

Figure B.1 The four views of IT architecture.
Figure B.2. The XYZ value chain.
Figure B.3. The information view.
Figure B.4. The applications view.

Figure B.5.   The target technology view.
Figure B.6.   The dispersion of target applications across computing levels.
Figure B.7.   COG to current organization matrix template.
Figure B.8.   COGs to user class affinity matrix template.
Figure B.9.   Target application to data grouping affinity matrix template.
Figure B.10.   Application characteristics template.
Figure B.11.   Target COGs to target application template.
Figure B.12.   Target application to target application (integration opportunity) template.
Figure B.13.   Target application to existing application (integration opportunities) template.
Figure B.14.   Target application to user class template.
Figure B.15.   Target application access by physical location template.
Figure B.16.   Target COGs to data grouping template.
Figure B.17.   Characteristics of information template.
Figure B.18.   Application to GAE affinity matrix template.
Figure B.19.   Client–server implementation types.
Figure B.20.   Target application to client–server implementation types.
Figure B.21.   Target application to levels of computing template.
Figure B.22.   Data groups to levels of computing template.

Chapter 5

Figure 5.1.   Project management is an important element of the foundation.

Chapter 6

Figure 6.1.   Adding business redesign to the organization.
Figure 6.2.   Sample business model diagram.
Figure 6.3.   Sample value chain diagram.

Appendix C

Figure C.1.   Event model excerpt.

Chapter 7

Figure 7.1.   Filling in the communications piece.
Figure 7.2.   Some important communication vehicles.
Figure 7.3.   A typical quality review process.
Figure 7.4.   The lessons learned should be captured and published.
Figure 7.5.   The e-bulletin board can be an important broadcast medium.
Figure 7.6.   Road shows take the message to the masses.
Figure 7.7.   The project coordination process.

Chapter 8

Figure 8.1.   Workforce inclusion is another important element.

Chapter 9

Figure 9.1.   The employee improvement program completes the picture.
Figure 9.2.   The CEI continuum.
Figure 9.3.   Sample performance measurement procedures.
Figure 9.4.   Workforce development is the foundation of other bottom-line improvements.

Appendix D

Figure D.1.   KCG's *Strategic Planning Methodology*™.

PREFACE

In the words of the great American philosopher Henry David Thoreau, it is time to "Simplify! Simplify! Simplify!"

This book is written out of a desire to quiet the noise that fills the air about advanced business strategy and management practices. So much conflicting advice is available about what it takes for organizations to be successful today that it is very easy to become confused. The messages are broadcast to us loudly and with pizzazz. "Sexy" buzzwords are introduced to an unsuspecting audience with bombast and bluster. What is one to do?

As a management consultant who has helped top-tier clients solve all kinds of problems over the years, I think the time has come to simplify the message. Tone down the volume and strip away the jargon. Indeed, it is time to get to the point.

These seven best practices are discussed in the book:

- Program-centric strategic planning
- Resilient IT architecture design
- Results-focused communications
- Portfolio-based project management
- Uninterrupted business redesign
- Cross-cultural workforce inclusion
- Continuous employee improvement

Why these seven? These best practices "cover the waterfront." They address the people, processes, and technology elements that comprise every enterprise. Yes, other important practices could have been considered. However, my research and personal experience points to these seven practices as the ones that truly make a difference. Without these firmly in place, an organization flounders. Indeed, these seven form the basis of an innovative management philosophy that, when driven from the top, transforms an organization from mediocrity to a venerable powerhouse.

The book begins with a vision for the future in Chapter 1. It uses *Your Company, Inc.*, a fictitious company, to drive home its points. However, *Your Company, Inc.* is just a metaphor. Indeed, the vision presented applies to any entity that chooses to conduct business in the early 21st century.

Chapter 2 offers 15 business principles. These principles should be embraced and instituted as a means of setting a solid foundation for implementing sweeping change within an enterprise.

It should be noted that these first two chapters, while establishing a firm underpinning for the remainder of the book, are geared toward capturing the imagination and intellect of an executive audience. The best practices discussed in subsequent chapters are written with practitioners and their managers in mind. The thought is that this book has something to offer both audiences, an important consideration, given that both audiences must act on the advice provided in order for an enterprise to realize the benefits of the message.

Chapter 3 covers program-centric strategic planning. It reveals how typical strategic planning can be transformed into a tool for improving top-line and bottom-line performance by redefining how it is implemented.

Chapter 4 focuses on resilient IT architecture design. It provides advice about how IT environments can be designed and built to bring their organizations to new levels of reliable responsiveness and speed-to-market while maximizing returns on technology investments.

Chapter 5 addresses portfolio-based project management. It demonstrates how this practice reduces risk and minimizes costs by introducing unprecedented rigor and discipline to the project planning and execution process.

Uninterrupted business redesign forms the basis of Chapter 6. It illustrates ways of extending standard business redesign practices into a continuous activity that serves to improve quality and enhance job satisfaction among staff.

Chapter 7 covers results-focused communications. It points out that internal and external communication practices must be enhanced and improved in order to position firms for increased effectiveness and profitability.

Chapter 8 demystifies cross-cultural workforce inclusion. It shows how diversity and inclusion programs can be used to increase shareholder value by celebrating personnel differences and leveraging the unique skills and talents that are uncovered.

Chapter 9 discusses continuous employee improvement. It explains how performance measurement/reward and training/development practices can be integrated to better manage, motivate, and develop the human resources needed for flawless execution.

The Postscript at the end of the book presents some final thoughts on the characteristics that make *Best Practices Enterprises*™ different from other organizations. It serves as a thoughtful reminder about what it takes to fast-track a company toward lasting success.

All the suggestions brought forth in the chapters come from experience. All the ideas and concepts presented here have been applied, tested, and refined through extensive research and work that I have personally done directly for and with my clients. Key points are driven home in each chapter through the use of chapter sidebars, which present stories about how today's organizations are applying the concepts discussed.

Additionally, excerpts from actual strategic planning, IT architecture, business redesign, and continuous employee improvement projects are presented in four appendices. Stripped of specific company references, these demonstrate how various multinational organizations have gone about the institutionalization of the best practices covered in the book.

May all these elements combine to provide you with all that is needed to help you establish a *Best Practices Enterprise*™. Enjoy the book.

James M. Kerr
Cromwell, Connecticut

ABOUT THE AUTHOR

 **James Kerr** is the managing partner at KCG, a leading management consulting firm, located in Cromwell, Connecticut, that specializes in assisting Fortune 500 firms with corporate visioning, scenario planning, mergers/acquisitions, process design, and enterprise reorganization.

Mr. Kerr is a highly respected management consultant with over 20 years of experience. He is best known for his corporate transformation, strategy formulation, and business redesign work. He has been published extensively in the media and has authored books for McGraw-Hill and John Wiley & Sons.

This leading expert is a sought-after speaker who also teaches graduate-level strategic planning courses within the Lally School of Management at Rensselaer Polytechnic Institute.

Although his primary focus has been advising larger global enterprises, such as Mitsui Sumitomo, The Home Depot, and AXA Financial, Mr. Kerr has also done significant work in the government sector, including the U.S. Department of Defense.

For more information about KCG visit *www.kerr-consulting-group.com* or reach Mr. Kerr directly at *jkerr@kerr-consulting-group.com*.

ACKNOWLEDGMENTS

Thank you to the people who made a difference during the writing of this book, especially:

The Kerrs, the Ruepps, the Buyaks, the Blanchards, and the Ryans, whose kind thoughts and actions always provide needed support and comfort;

Joe Mooney and Ed Kelly, who seem to derive true joy in keeping me honest;

Brian and Kelly McCarthy, who regularly reignite my Jukes obsession;

Drew Gierman, who believed in the project from the start and pushed me to make it better;

Alex Brown, who offered assistance early on;

The Sugar Cube Café, for the table in the back;

All my friends in Cromwell, particularly the Soccer Moms and Dads, who helped remind me that there is more to life than writing a book; and

Irene, Dylan, and Haley, who sacrifice and make mine all worthwhile.

Free value-added materials from
the Download Resource Center at www.jross.com

At J. Ross Publishing we are committed to providing today's professional with practical, hands-on tools that enhance the learning experience and give readers an opportunity to apply what they have learned. That is why we offer free ancillary materials available for download on this book and all participating Web Added Value™ publications. These online resources may include interactive versions of material that appears in the book or supplemental templates, worksheets, models, plans, case studies, proposals, spreadsheets and assessment tools, among other things. Whenever you see the WAV™ symbol in any of our publications it means bonus materials accompany the book and are available from the Web Added Value™ Download Resource Center at www.jrosspub.com.

Downloads available for *The Best Practices Enterprise™: A Guide to Achieving Sustainable World-Class Performance* consist of free tips for effective best practices implementation and business transformation. Downloads are available from the Web Added Value™ Download Resource Center at www.jrosspub.com.

THE BEST PRACTICES ENTERPRISE™—A NEW VISION FOR A NEW ERA

The most pathetic person in the world is someone who has sight, but has no vision.

—Helen Keller

It is the dawn of a new era—one that will be marked by the establishment of a type of company that is substantially different from the ones that evolved out of the Industrial Age. The businesses that will thrive in the new era will be characterized by optimized organizational structures, enhanced product and service delivery models, and unmatched market reach. Some of these most successful companies will advance from today's existing organizations. Others have yet to be started.

Nonetheless, these businesses will operate in a state of continual transformation. These organizations will be limber, ever prepared to do what it takes to respond to a rapidly changing and often tumultuous marketplace. They will be quick, nimble, interconnected, diverse, service-minded, and virtually independent of physical location.

The Best Practices Enterprise™ is the name given to such organizations. It is *The Best Practices Enterprise*™ that will dominate industry throughout the 21st century. Wouldn't it be great to ensure that your company is one of the dominant players in the marketplace? This can be achieved. It begins with a little imagination.

IMAGINE: *YOUR COMPANY, INC.*

What does *Your Company, Inc.* look like? How does it work? Take a moment and imagine …

*   *   *

The company, *Your Company, Inc.*, is entirely interconnected to all of its stakeholders. Customers, suppliers, distributors, bankers, investors, and employees form an immense web that embodies the "enterprise." The hard boundaries that separated these entities in years past have all but disappeared. Instead, there are networks of interdependent parts, connected through technology. This "inter-

---

BEST PRACTICES BUSINESS IN ACTION

A Store-in-a-Box Strategy for FNAC

FNAC is the leading French retailer of books, music, and consumer electronics in Europe. Part of the Pinaul–Printemps–Redoute Group, the 20th largest retailer in Europe, FNAC has over 70 stores across the continent (and in Brazil and Taiwan) and a rather sophisticated e-commerce operation. Since its inception in 1954, the company has been known as "the ambassador of culture," and its broad network of stores helps to make it so.

In an effort to continue to grow aggressively internationally, the firm developed a program called FNAC-in-a-Box. The strategy establishes a common IT infrastructure, standard operating procedures, and a common organization design to be implemented in each store that the company opens.

By using the same plan (i.e., "box"), FNAC ensures that each store will open quickly, employ the same best practices, and easily tie into the company's centralized logistics and administrative operations.

The FNAC stores in Milan and Geneva were the first to use the approach. Opened for business within a month of each other, these successes show that FNAC can enter a new country, open new stores, and link them back to the home office operations within months.

FNAC is a *Best Practices Enterprise*™ pioneer that shows that even large, global enterprises can harvest business processes that allow them to be nimble and quick.

Source: Based on "FNAC Reinvests in Retek to Support Multi-National Strategy," www.retek.com, 2004.

BEST PRACTICES BUSINESS IN ACTION
Speed Counts at Hartness International

Surely, speed does count at Hartness International. The Greenville, South Carolina, company makes case packers, which are high-speed machines that load bottles of consumables, such as beer and soda, into cartons for shipment to retail outlets. It is committed to providing its 5000 customers around the globe with world-class service.

Time is money for Hartness customers. Problems with case-packing machines can bring an entire bottling line "to its knees." A downed machine can cost the average customer nearly a quarter of a million dollars a day in lost revenues. So, getting a Hartness technician to a machine in need of repair has always been the firm's highest priority.

In response to this need for speed, Hartness International developed the HERO system—Hartness Error Recording Online. HERO's four tiny video cameras capture and log video, triggered by an error event. Easily mounted in the most difficult locations on a packing line, the system has the ability to maintain video operation histories that can be utilized to diagnose both chronic and intermittent problems.

Customers such as Heineken, Coca-Cola, and Anheuser-Busch use HERO's remote access and Internet capabilities to tie in Hartness engineers with in-house technicians. This enables immediate expert servicing of machines from anywhere in the world.

Clearly, Hartness International is a fine example of the *Best Practices Era* evolution. Hartness realizes that speed counts and immediate response to customer needs is essential to future success. Its leadership has demonstrated that it is willing to invest time and money today to be better prepared for tomorrow.

Source: Based on "Every product line needs a HERO," *Hartness Hi-Lites Online Newsletter*, Volume 1, 1st Quarter 2003.

connectedness" pays dividends by improving process efficiencies on the supply-side of the business and by enhancing customer loyalty on the demand-side.

As a result, *Your Company, Inc.* is a lot more nimble than it used to be. It has picked up the pace. It has learned how to respond quickly to changes in the marketplace by streamlining operations and business processes through continuous business reengineering activities. With a focus on people, processes, and automated systems, a type of workflow fluidity has been founded that has been unheard of until now. In fact, it has refined process redesign so well that it can change workflow "on a dime" and introduce new products faster than ever before.

After all, speed is important because the producer/consumer dynamic has changed, too. Customers have become more demanding. They want what they want when they want it—and they will accept nothing less. In response, *Your Company, Inc.* has evolved from mass production to mass customization. It has been a matter of survival. If you cannot figure out how to meet your customers' specific needs, they will find someone who can.

Yet, product design is not the only element of the value proposition that needs to be tailored. The delivery of impeccable customer service has become one of the key differentiators for *Your Company, Inc.* Today, the firm does not tolerate any behavior that is inconsistent with delivering world-class customer service to its customers. If a customer's needs are not put first, you simply do not last at *Your Company, Inc.*

The push toward mass customization and unsurpassed service delivery has led *Your Company, Inc.* to become very efficient as well. In fact, it has developed a clear and distinct concentration on developing and advancing those capabilities that set it apart in the marketplace.

BEST PRACTICES BUSINESS IN ACTION

Business Is Picking Up (and Delivering) at Takeout Taxi

Do you ever crave Thai food when your spouse wants a pizza? What do you do? Do not fret. Your problem is solved. Just pick up the phone and call Takeout Taxi. Takeout Taxi can deliver an order of Tom Ka Gai soup for you and a pepperoni and onion pie for your spouse.

Takeout Taxi was one of the first to anticipate what has become a major trend in society—people want to eat restaurant meals at home—and they want them delivered. Because not all restaurants offer this service, Takeout Taxi saw a niche to exploit by becoming a delivery service for local restaurateurs in the area. A business was born.

Takeout Taxi, a licensed brand name of Brand Solutions, LLC, has been in operation since the early 1990s. It operates in 18 major markets in the United States—including Boston, Chicago, Los Angeles, and Washington, D.C. Last year, Takeout Taxi's gross revenue was over $23 million. That is a lot of takeout!

What makes Takeout Taxi different from other companies that offer similar home delivery services, such as Domino's Pizza, is that Takeout Taxi is a customized distributor of restaurant foods. The others are actually mass distributors of the products that they make (e.g., Domino's delivers only Domino's pizza). Takeout Taxi will deliver foods from a variety of restaurants in the area—customizing their offering to your cravings.

Takeout Taxi is a great *Best Practices Business Model* because it focuses on the customer and delivers what customers want when they want it. Certainly, more businesses will be adopting this kind of "customized service" approach in the future.

Source: Based on information derived from the Takeout Taxi website, www.takeout-taxi.com, November 26, 2005.

BEST PRACTICES BUSINESS IN ACTION
Is There a Doctor in the House?

Recent advances in telemedicine are providing solid examples of location independence at work. The ability of a physician to assist colleagues from afar through the use of technology is a cost-effective solution for the challenge of providing long-distance care without any compromise to quality. NEC's revolutionary TeleDoc 5000 system is an innovative example of telemedicine technology in action.

NEC's TeleDoc 5000 system is fully integrated, self-contained, and portable. It facilitates efficient two-way, audio/visual interaction between medical specialists and physicians who are on-site with patients—helping general practitioners and rural hospitals to maintain their patients' care on-site by providing access to specialists from around the world.

The TeleDoc 5000 system is a virtual "telemedicine-in-a-box" solution. It comes fully equipped with everything that is needed to provide remote medical support, including:

- High-resolution room camera with pan, zoom, and autofocus
- High-speed data port for direct connection to an X-ray scanner
- Low-speed data ports for transmission of computer files
- VHS video cassette recorder for video documentation of examination
- Hands-free microphone
- Thirteen-inch high-resolution monitor for displaying the local images
- Nine-inch monitor for viewing the consulting physician at the remote facility

The TeleDoc 5000 system can also be extended to connect with many other standard telemedicine devices, such as electronic stethoscopes, EKGs, and electronic exam cameras—enabling expert practitioners to provide remote assistance on such procedures as arthroscopy, laparoscopy, cystoscopy, hysteroscopy, bronchoscopy, pelviscopy, laryngoscopy, colonoscopy, gastroscopy, ureteroscopy, and sinescopy.

With the TeleDoc 5000 and systems like it, medical specialists are entering into the age of best practices in telemedicine—and that is good for everyone.

Source: Based on information provided by NEC America, Inc., 1555 W. Walnut Hill Lane, Irving, TX.

In so doing, the company has become deliberate about forging new relationships with best-in-class vendors who can oversee those parts of the business that provide no discernable differentiation. In this way, *Your Company, Inc.* has directed its energies to those things that really matter and has let mundane activities be managed by outside specialists who do those things efficiently and cost-effectively.

Similarly, it has had to flip outdated assumptions about its fixed and variable cost structure "on their ears." By outsourcing the mundane, *Your Company, Inc.*

BEST PRACTICES BUSINESS IN ACTION

Merrill Lynch Is Bullish on Telecommuting

Merrill Lynch is a classic example of where business is heading in the 21st century. Merrill Lynch has established a program to help employees prepare to be truly effective "telecommuters."

The comprehensive training program covers major issues that can influence the effectiveness of a telecommuter, including:

1. How to stay in the loop at work while working at home—Merrill Lynch requires most of its telecommuters to spend at least 1 day a week in the office.
2. How to create a solid home-based work environment—Merrill Lynch spends about $7000 per person to equip a telecommuter's home office.
3. How to work remotely—Merrill Lynch has three simulation labs across the country where prospective telecommuters can practice telecommuting.

Hundreds of staff members have participated in the training sessions, but getting in the program is no sure thing. A prospective telecommuter must apply for the privilege by submitting a detailed proposal that describes the *how, when, where*, and *why* that make telecommuting a compelling proposition for both the telecommuter and the company. Training begins once applicants are screened and approved by their management—then, everyone spends at least 2 weeks in one of the simulation labs.

The Merrill Lynch program is just one of many that are sure to spring up as organizations face the realities of doing business in the *Best Practices Era*.

Source: Based on "Merrill Lynch works—at home" by Lisa Chadderdon, *Fast Company*, April/May 1998, pp. 70–72.

has become a more "variable" business enterprise—one that can scale to size as needed. In other words, it pays for only the capabilities that it needs at the time. It limits fixed and capital cost investments to those things that are absolutely essential to establishing market differentiation. Overhead is kept low and flexibility is enhanced when a firm "pays as it goes."

As a direct result, *Your Company, Inc.* has diminished its thirst for "bricks and mortar." It has found that the physical location of the business is far less important than its logical locale within its interconnected network. Customers are doing business with the company from across the globe in a virtual market. Similarly, workers are contributing their knowledge and labor from the comfort of their living rooms (whenever feasible).

In fact, this new-found corporate flexibility has given way to a different type of worker population as well. There are far more independent contractors, temporary workers, and consultants in place than ever before. *Your Company, Inc.* has found that the use of "free agents" has improved its ability to ramp-up and size-down as needed. It has also allowed the firm to improve its "organizational knowledge" without having to incur the cost of cultivating it from within.

In turn, this new business model has introduced workforce diversity in epic proportions. It is a "cross-border" and "cross-culture" company. Workers from all types of ethnic, educational, and experiential backgrounds now inhabit the workplace—promoting new ways of "thinking and doing" never before imagined in business. As a result, the corporate culture at *Your Company, Inc.* is constantly evolving and changing for the better. It is fun and exciting to go to work.

Consequently, a new project management mentality has materialized within *Your Company, Inc.* The company has found that work is best managed as a portfolio of projects and programs rather than as a set of tasks arranged around

BEST PRACTICES BUSINESS IN ACTION

Diversity in Action in San Diego

The city of San Diego takes the issue of workforce diversity very seriously. It has a diversity program underway and keeps a full-time team in place to oversee its execution. The city even addresses workforce diversity in its mission statement, including this passage:

... *To create an environment where differences are valued and all employees are a productive part of a high-performing team delivering services to the community.*

That is a very impressive and forward-thinking statement for an organization to make, let alone a municipal government that we so often consider old and stodgy. But San Diego's city government is not a typical city government.

The city's strategic plan calls for extending its diversity program by:

- Incorporating a norms and values assessment on employee performance reviews
- Designing an employee selection process that will help create a representative workforce for the city
- Changing policies and procedures to encourage inclusive behaviors in the workplace
- Developing a communications strategy that will better recognize workers and departments across the city for their inclusive acts

All these initiatives go a long way toward establishing the change that the city's government must make to prepare for even broader workforce diversity in the future.

What is happening in San Diego is a model for all organizations to survey as they begin to address the implications of a broadly diverse workforce and a growing free agent society—both compelling best practices business trends.

Source: Based on "Strategies for success: the San Diego story" by Margaret Blackburn White, *The Diversity Factor*, Summer 1996, Volume 4, Number 4, pp. 2–10.

a hierarchy of departments—which has become ineffective in overseeing cross-company strategic initiatives as the worker population grows more diverse and transient.

The internal strategic dynamics of *Your Company, Inc.* have changed as well. Fueled by the pervasive energy of the new global era, the company has conceived a fresh vision for the future—instituting a new set of business principles aimed at redefining the way the enterprise should be run.

Strategic planning has been institutionalized. It is an ongoing process that keeps track of all of the activities going on within the company. It is no longer something that is done once a year when it is time to dole out the annual departmental budgets. After all, in an environment of rapid change, there must be some semblance of order or chaos will result. The strategic plan keeps it all together.

BEST PRACTICES BUSINESS IN ACTION

METRO Group: The Store of the Future Takes Hold in Germany

In April 2003, the METRO Group opened the "store of the future" in Rhineberg, Germany—and shopping for groceries may never be the same again.

The Metro Group is one of the largest trading and retail groups in the world. With over 2300 stores across 28 countries, it has a presence around the globe. Ever challenged by the thirst for internationalization and differentiation, the company continues to seek out new ways of doing business. The "store of the future" is an answer to the challenge.

The Rhineberg store uses radio frequency identification (RFID) technology to track products through their entire life cycle—from production through inventory tracking on shelves to sale to the consumer.

For example, RFID-tagged items are placed on pallets and scanned upon leaving the warehouse, and shipping data are sent to the store manager for review. Upon receipt at the store, the pallets are scanned again and any discrepancies are immediately generated on a report. Anything missing or damaged can be replaced through a follow-up order.

But it does not stop there. The "store of the future" also features these capabilities:

- RFID-equipped shopping carts monitor customer length of stay.
- The system triggers item replenishment when low volume is indicated.
- The system flags misplaced items for restocking.

The METRO Group fully expects that its Rhineberg store will improve the customer shopping experience (by having the best and freshest items available all the time), while enhancing operating efficiencies (through automation) for the store.

We can fully expect that the store of the future serves as a solid example of a best practices business in the making.

Source: Based on "METRO Group's future store takes German public by storm—thanks to wireless e-business on demand technology," www.ibm.com, 2004.

BEST PRACTICES BUSINESS IN ACTION

Enhancing the Employee Experience at British American Tobacco, plc (BAT Group)

The BAT Group is the world's second-largest quoted tobacco company, with a 15% world market share and over 40 billion packs of cigarettes shipped annually.

Its Mexico division, located in Monterrey, was challenged by employee turnover and difficulty in motivating staff to make the changes needed to keep the company competitive. One of the steps taken by the BAT Group to improve communications and enhance employee relations was to create an employee portal.

Accessible from both the company's website and BAT's intranet, the employee portal provides staff with:

- "Chat" and "forum" functions—where opinions can be voiced and suggestions offered
- Up-to-the-minute company information—effectively sharing business strategies, performance goals, and corporate communications
- Work–family balancing and quality-of-life articles—aimed at offering insight and perspective on life's challenges

In the near future, the BAT Group intends to extend e-learning capabilities to staff via the portal.

Clearly, the company is transforming its performance through knowledge sharing and the innovative use of communication vehicles—a *Best Practices Era* business development that cannot be ignored.

Source: Based on "British American Tobacco/ BAT Mexico: employee portal," www.accenture.com, 2004.

The use of automation to compete has matured immensely. *Your Company, Inc.* has formalized and now aggressively manages an information systems architecture plan. The architecture provides a blueprint for the types of information, systems, and technologies needed to support the business.

The adoption of industry standard technology tool suites has enabled a new-found level of resiliency not attainable in years past. Systems can be updated, moved, and installed quicker than ever before. New automated capabilities can be put into place seamlessly by plugging in new components and retiring old ones as their usefulness diminishes over time. This newly found flexibility has proven to be a real boon when compared with the time (often measured in years) that such changes required before the architecture was in place. In fact, standards-based development has resulted in the establishment of a highly stable and hardy set of automated systems—ones that can be modified quickly and withstand computing threats of all kinds.

A focus on business communication has emerged as well. Solid communication vehicles have been put into place to ensure that everyone involved in any way with the business is kept abreast of what is going on and has access to everyone in the firm. It is the only way to ensure that *Your Company, Inc.* is leveraging all its resources to the fullest (as far flung as they have become).

Training and education has become a major theme for the organization. A continuous employee improvement program has been established. It centers on behavior modification through training and performance measurement in which business results become the only focus, not some sort of unintended by-product of the work performed.

An inclusion effort that addresses the workforce diversity challenge has sprung up as well. It has become a major influence within the company. As a result, *Your Company, Inc.* has been able to develop and retain staff from around the globe, simultaneously building sustainable "corporate knowledge" within the firm.

Of course, with all of this the corporate bureaucracy that has held strong since the industrial revolution is gone. *Your Company, Inc.* cannot afford to have layers of managers managing layers of managers. More importantly, the company can no longer afford the sluggishness that became endemic with the bureaucracy. It replaced the chain-of-command model with a team-based one that empowers workers to make procedural adjustments as needed in response to market demands.

Clearly, *Your Company, Inc.* has become a world leader in its markets by anticipating the future and preparing itself to flourish there. The company has never been better positioned to weather demand swings, market fluctuations, and economic downturns—wherever and however they arise. It is a force to be reckoned with.

* * *

If Your Company, Inc. existed as imagined, would you want to be part of it? From time to time throughout the book, reference will be made to the vision that has been laid out for *Your Company, Inc.*, but for now, it suffices to say that with hard work and perseverance any business can become a dominant player in the global marketplace.

Let us explore how.

THE BEST PRACTICES ENTERPRISE™ PHILOSOPHY

So how does a company position itself to respond to the changes that the new era holds in store? Certainly, an attempt can be made to define the next "big thing." Yet, if that attempt fails, and most of the time such attempts do fail, the value that stockholders seek will not be delivered. Instead, why not return focus to the fun-

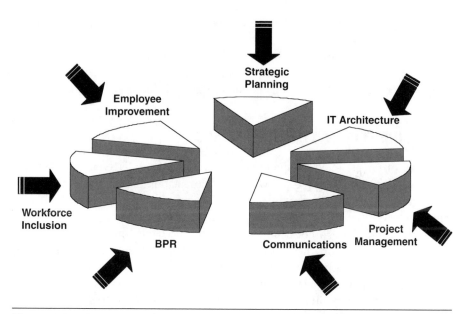

Figure 1.1   Fitting all the best practices together is our challenge.

damentals, much like a slumping athlete would when trying to return to world-class form?

By embracing what might be called a *"Best Practices Enterprise™ philosophy"* that focuses attention on sound fundamentals, businesses can begin to introduce new programs, and extend existing programs, that position them to be nimble and quick while still growing and evolving into broad-reaching and highly profitable organizations.

In this book, the seven most essential best practices are identified. There are no silver bullets among them, but together they form an indispensable strategic underpinning that can make the difference between long-term success and failure for any organization within the new epoch.

The seven business programs that constitute *The Best Practices Enterprise™* philosophy include:

- Program-centric strategic planning
- Resilient IT architecture design
- Results-focused communications
- Portfolio-based project management
- Uninterrupted business redesign
- Cross-cultural workforce inclusion
- Continuous employee improvement

As Figure 1.1 suggests, these seven business practices, when institutionalized, fit together seamlessly.

There are certainly other best practices that could have been considered. However, these seven are the most important. They effectively cover all of the people, processes, and technology elements that make up every organization.

A RECIPE FOR LASTING SUCCESS

In a time of unparalleled competition, where all the rules have been broken and the contestants are looking for new ways of devastating their rivals, it is refreshing to recognize that an important part of the solutions sought can be found in the fundamentals.

Business leaders do not need to spend their precious time searching for the "new and exciting," they need focus on the essential, elementary best practices that will provide a solid platform for identifying and, more importantly, implementing the breakthrough strategies needed for competing in this millennium.

The chapters that follow will provide a recipe for success. It is up to all of us to go through the effort of putting these ingredients together and making it happen for our organizations. A collection of business principles are presented next. They are of irrefutable importance and lend purpose and meaning to the best practices programs that encompass the rest of the book.

Let us begin our exploration of what it takes to improve performance and deliver lasting results within today's organizations.

* * *

BEST PRACTICES BUSINESS PRINCIPLES

*Clearly, **Your Company, Inc.** has become a world leader in its markets by anticipating the future and preparing itself to flourish there. The company has never been better positioned to weather demand swings, market fluctuations, and economic downturns—wherever and however they arise. It is a force to be reckoned with.*

Although today's global business environment is fraught with unprecedented challenges, it provides organizations with one tremendous opportunity—the opportunity to reinvent. With a new business epoch upon us, existing organizational models, operating policies, workflows, trading practices, reporting structures, and even the goods and services offered should all be rethought and redefined.

By considering the best practices presented in this book, organizations can choose to exploit the opportunity to change and drive their enterprises to unparalleled success. Those that choose not to reinvent themselves will fall behind.

Let us examine how businesses can begin to position themselves for the continual transformation that is required today. It all starts with the fashioning and expression of a new strategic agenda—one that is both stirring and bold.

A NEW AGENDA FOR THE NEW ERA

What follows is a set of *Best Practices Business Principles*. They frame the new agenda. Indeed, they encompass it. If adopted, these business principles will

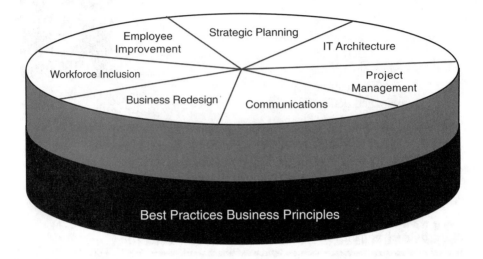

Figure 2.1   The business principles form a solid foundation for the best practices.

guide direction and encourage the behaviors that are needed to deliver unmatched performance. As suggested by Figure 2.1, they form the foundation for the best practices that will be discussed throughout the remainder of the book.

The business principles include:

1. The *Best Practices Enterprise*™ will place "laser-like" focus on establishing a work environment that supports continuous transformation.
2. Processes will be broadened to include all related responsibilities and tasks, free of existing organization design or "chain of command."
3. Processes will be designed to be independent of current work locations and physical plant.
4. Strategic planning will be a continuously performed process, and all new initiatives will be evaluated via this process before inclusion in the strategic plan.
5. All work to be done within the firm must be included in the strategic plan before commencing.
6. Work will be managed as a portfolio of projects and programs.
7. The information technology environment will be architected with resilience and flawless integration in mind.
8. The *Best Practices Enterprise*™ will aggressively leverage the emerging free agent market.

9. Diversity and inclusion efforts will be aimed exclusively at establishing a culture in which individual differences among workers are recognized as valuable ingredients in achieving the best business outcomes for the organization.
10. Communication will be recognized as a vital process that must be managed deliberately.
11. With increasing business variability in mind, the work environment will be constantly monitored to identify opportunities to outsource routine activities to best-of-breed vendors.
12. The organization will seek to establish new types of vendor relationships that clearly define mutual gain for the parties involved.
13. The *Best Practices Enterprise*™ will adopt "continuous employee improvement" behaviors.
14. Performance measurement programs will focus on results and not effort.
15. A team-based management model will be adopted by the company to enhance the ability to better respond to emerging market opportunities.

Keep in mind that these business principles are nothing more than statements of executive management's preferences regarding the way in which an enterprise should conduct its affairs in the execution of its mission. Once fully institutionalized, these principles must be considered "rules of the road" for how personnel should plan, manage, and work within the concern. Together they forge the agenda needed to introduce the level of rigor and discipline that is required to reinvent the organization.

Each business principle is discussed in more detail below. The *rationale* and *implications* for each of them are provided. A principle's rationale is the "reason" why it is important to an enterprise, while its implications can be considered the "price" an organization must pay to realize its benefits.

THE BUSINESS PRINCIPLES

PRINCIPLE 1

The *Best Practices Enterprise*™ will place "laser-like" focus on establishing a work environment that supports continuous transformation.

Rationale

Today's organizations must direct all their resources and energy to instituting a work environment that supports continuous transformation. The competitive landscape of the early 21st century will allow nothing less. It must be able to change workflow "on a dime" and introduce new products faster than ever before.

But change, for the sake of change, is not how the game is won. Long-term success in the marketplace comes from placing emphasis on, and aggressively managing toward establishing, a workplace that is nimble and capable of swift response.

With that said, senior management must focus its attention on deploying all their organization's internal resources (i.e., people, processes, and technology) on creating the proper corporate culture for *perpetual* change.

Implications

- Internal operating efficiency must be regarded as an important means of enhancing the bottom line. Nonessential activities that drain vital energy and internal capacity must be eliminated. Initiatives that reduce costs, improve the workflow, and leverage technology must be introduced.

- The *Best Practices Enterprise™* must evaluate the current level of customer service and satisfaction. Programs must be developed that identify best practice techniques in use within the company and those used in the industry. These programs must incorporate measurement and feedback systems that continually monitor customer service levels.

- Service levels between internal customers must be identified and improved with a focus on the common objective of superior service to external customers.

- A method for performing uninterrupted business redesign (U-BPR) must be introduced and implemented in order to position the firm for perpetual change.

- Staff must be trained in the firm's preferred U-BPR methodology.

- Finally, early successes must be broadly recognized and celebrated within the organization in order to encourage the cultural transformation that lasting change will bring.

PRINCIPLE 2

Processes will be broadened to include all related responsibilities and tasks, free of existing organization design or "chain of command."

Rationale

Today, work within the company is delineated by business unit and geographical location. A specific type of work is performed in one business unit and is then passed to the next unit for further piecework, much as in an assembly line.

The assembly line, given the power of today's technology, is becoming an unnecessary constraint. The many hand-offs make the assembly-line approach an expensive, time-consuming, and error-prone proposition.

The days when the "it is not my job" attitude was acceptable are long past. Rather, the time has come for staff to assume the responsibility for getting the job done, regardless of position, organization chart, or chain-of-command.

An organization's success in rebuilding the way work is done rests on defining business processes that have no organizational boundaries and on preparing personnel to "do whatever it takes" to get the job done.

The *Best Practices Enterprise*™ must evolve to this type of environment in order to remain competitive.

Implications

- Processes will need to be reviewed and redefined, independent of current organizational boundaries. Emphasis will need to be placed on performing the "whole job" instead of only specific pieces. Artificial boundaries that promote a "silo" mentality need to be eliminated.
- Jobs will be redefined. All attendant responsibilities and commitments related to performing the "whole job" will need to be folded into job specifications.
- Managers will need education on how to manage the process to optimize results rather than manage the activities of people performing the work. The game is won by gaining the expected results, not by micromanaging the work of each employee.
- Projects aimed at reengineering selected business processes will be necessary to ensure that "best practices" and other quality standards are designed into new processes.
- U-BPR strategies will need to be adopted to continue the improvement effort on an ongoing basis.
- Training personnel is a must. Specifically, educating employees about new organization designs, process definition, and job responsibilities is essential in gaining buy-in and reducing the feelings of friction or alienation that often come with change.

PRINCIPLE 3

Processes will be designed to be independent of current work locations and physical plant.

Rationale

In today's world, technology enables an organization to ignore geographical distances in the performance of work activities. Individuals can participate remotely on work teams without much impact on performance (except for the effect that lack of human contact may cause).

This capability provides management with increased flexibility in defining the company's work environment. Remote work locations can be reviewed for ways to better meet customer needs. Individual contributors can be given the latitude to work close to their "customers" wherever they may be.

The ability to better respond to changes in the marketplace increases as geographical boundaries diminish. Business processes need not be limited by geography.

Implications

- Processes will need to be reviewed and reengineered as necessary.
- There will be a fundamental shift in the way personnel think about work. The functional perspective that is prevalent today should give way to recognizing that there are few physical boundaries for business processes and that the work is better executed and managed by focusing on processes rather than functions.
- The traditional organizational structure will require adjustment to further accommodate remote personnel. Today's command and control structure should be updated to allow greater flexibility in managing personnel and monitoring their performance.
- Management's roles must change in this more flexible work environment as well. Managers must be prepared to become less directive and to fine-tune the coaching skills necessary to motivate geographically dispersed personnel.
- There will be a clear need for training every employee (whether temporary or permanent) in the fundamentals of business processes. Personnel should come to understand that business processes are *virtual* by nature and that *where* work is performed is far less important than getting the work *done right the first time*.

PRINCIPLE 4

Strategic planning will be a continuously performed process and all new initiatives will be evaluated via this process before inclusion in the strategic plan.

Rationale

This principle is an important means of turning the widely accepted and outdated idea about strategic planning as being nothing more than an annual budget planning exercise "on its ear." Instead, this principle calls for strategic planning to become a constant, continuous process that ensures that businesses are able to adjust and evolve as competitive necessities dictate.

Further, by embracing this notion, the organization is clearly recognizing the value of the *Program-Centric Strategic Planning Best Practice* as a means for evaluating future business options and investment choices (while it further recognizes the strategic plan as the proper placeholder for "all things strategic").

Finally, the strategic plan documentation element ensures that the *Best Practices Enterprise*™ has an "organizational memory" that can be referenced in the future as the individual's memories of what took place have faded.

Implications

- The program-centric strategic planning process must be documented and published.
- Personnel (at all levels) must be trained in the planning process and be required to apply it in all that they do.
- A communications program must be put in place to ensure that all staff members fully understand the planning process and their role in it.
- A strategic planning office must be staffed in order to administer the planning process and ensure its integrity.
- Because of the procedural and cultural change that this principle represents, the management team must be prepared for some resistance among their ranks and be willing to work to keep each other *honest* as the new planning behaviors are being learned.

PRINCIPLE 5

All work to be done within the firm must be included in the strategic plan before commencing.

Rationale

This principle ensures that the company makes certain that all initiatives (to be staffed and funded in the future) are fully understood by the management team and that unintended organizational conflicts are actively considered as part of priority-setting across the firm.

What is more, the enterprise is much more effectively positioned to aggressively manage its resources and the harvesting of expected project and program benefits—thereby reducing the possibilities of squandering precious resources on ill-conceived and faulty ideas.

This comprehensive and objective way of dealing with potential projects/program opportunities will yield benefits far beyond the obvious as increased discipline and rigor extend throughout the organization.

Implications

- The planning process must define what constitutes a project or program within the concern.
- The program-centric strategic planning process must include a means for nominating new projects and programs for consideration by the executive team.
- Provisions must be incorporated into the process to ensure executive steering committee participation in project selection and priority setting.
- Organizational elements, such as weekly project coordination meetings and project reviews, must be put into place to ensure that project work is properly harmonized within the company.
- The ever-changing strategic plan must be communicated regularly throughout the enterprise.

PRINCIPLE 6

Work will be managed as a portfolio of projects and programs.

Rationale

A project-oriented culture is an essential underpinning of the *Best Practices Enterprise*™. The need for quick response and high-quality service delivery requires that organizations be positioned to implement new capabilities and modify operations "on a dime."

Managing work as a hierarchy of departments has inundated the organization in political red tape and delay. Clearly, organizing work into a portfolio of projects and programs reduces the obstacles to quick response by offering a different perspective on the way results can be achieved.

Also, *Program-Centric Strategic Planning* and *Resilient IT Architecture Design Best Practices* call for new strategic initiatives to be organized into a portfolio to best streamline plan administration and expedite project execution.

Implications

- Portfolio-based project management best practice methods must be selected and put into place in order to ensure the smooth implementation of this concept.
- The firm should be deliberate in establishing a common project management language and training personnel in its use.
- Project management skills must be developed and nurtured in order to fully realize the potential of portfolio-based project management.
- An awareness program will be necessary to expose all the firm's personnel to this new way of organizing and performing work within the company.
- This new work model represents a dramatic departure from the current work paradigm (that promotes functional boundaries as a way of partitioning and managing work). Management must be prepared to provide the counseling and support that will be required by their staff members as they make the transition.

PRINCIPLE 7

The information technology environment will be architected with resilience and flawless integration in mind.

Rationale

The *Best Practices Enterprise*™ demands that IT architectures be thoughtfully designed with resilience built in. The highly competitive marketplace requires that systems be capable of rapid change and extensibility.

Further, by assuming a philosophy of "building once and using anywhere," firms can avoid the cost of creating and maintaining multiple versions of systems across their various work locations. Applications that are designed independently of technical platforms can be ported to new environments as needs arise, with little or no modification—resulting in minimal interruption to business operations.

This level of application flexibility will provide the company with the capacity to "move" applications to the least expensive processing environment—reducing costs and lessening the company's reliance on any particular vendor or product suite.

Implications

- A standard IT architecture development methodology must be chosen and implemented within the concern.
- The company must define a standards suite with which its technology platforms and applications portfolios (including developed, packaged, or customized software) must conform.
- Personnel involved in application acquisition/development must be educated in the IT architecture methodology and its corresponding standards.
- An application review process must be put into place and used to ensure that any automated system that is implemented meets the resilience needs of the organization and that it will easily integrate into the rest of the IT architecture.

PRINCIPLE 8

The *Best Practices Enterprise*™ will aggressively leverage the emerging free agent market.

Rationale

Over 30 million Americans work independently, and the number is growing. People like the autonomy that comes with self-employment. Clearly, some of the "best and brightest" prefer it. *Best Practices Enterprises*™ need to face these facts and plan accordingly.

Further, the use of contracted talent is a key ingredient to establishing needed agility. Hiring *what is needed, when needed* is how the game is won in a highly competitive marketplace, such as the one in place today.

Implications

- Firms must make a conscious effort to establish programs aimed at creating a culture that attracts, develops, and retains quality, free agent personnel.
- Permanent staff must be made aware of the trends taking shape in the employment market and the company's desire to leverage the opportunities that exist there.

- Free agent personnel must be trained in the organization's operating policies, procedures, and quality standards so that they can get up to speed quickly and deliver desired results.
- The *Best Practices Enterprise*™ management team must promote this culture shift through its actions and be prepared to actively manage the enterprise through this transition.

PRINCIPLE 9

Diversity and inclusion efforts will be aimed exclusively at establishing a culture in which individual differences among workers are recognized as valuable ingredients in achieving the best business outcomes for the organization.

Rationale

Many organizations have adopted a "color blindness" and "gender neutrality" that seems to have the effect of ignoring, rather than recognizing and leveraging, individual employee differences. This has to change in order to position firms for success in the emerging global marketplace.

The necessity of conducting business on a worldwide scale requires organizations to rethink the old paradigm and recast it in such a way as to celebrate individual differences among a broadly diverse workforce and to leverage these differences as a means of gaining an edge over the competition.

Implications

- A diversity and inclusion program should be established as a means of jump-starting the company's desired cultural transition.
- The management team must commit to identifying desired outcomes from the program and begin to fold those outcomes into the performance measurement process.
- A roll-out effort must be developed and executed as a means of raising staff awareness and assisting the concern in learning new ways of working.
- Correspondingly, existing recruiting and retention programs should be reexamined and improved in ways that support the diversity/inclusion imperative.
- Beyond the typical human resources department, the organization should establish an executive office/officer to oversee continued diversity and inclusion efforts as a means of demonstrating senior commitment to the program.

PRINCIPLE 10

Communication is recognized as an important process that must be managed deliberately.

Rationale

Communication is a "trouble spot" within most *Best Practices Enterprises*™. Important company news and information are not provided to staff consistently or in a standard way, sometimes leading to misunderstanding and confusion.

With this said, effort must be aimed at establishing a comprehensive communications program—one in which resources are invested in planning and institutionalizing the appropriate communication mechanisms across the organization so that they are readily understood and used.

Implications

- A communication strategy should be developed. The strategy should include the definition of the communication devices that the company must implement to ensure that information is properly conveyed across all levels of the organization.
- Existing and new technology must be utilized to deliver business communication.
- Once the communication devices are identified and in place, an awareness program aimed at training personnel in their proper use will be necessary.
- Every employee will need to have access to the communication devices put into place by the organization.
- The management team must seek to hire, develop, and retain staff members who possess superior communication skills.
- An officer of the enterprise must be charged with overseeing the implementation and ongoing nurturing of the resultant communication strategy.

PRINCIPLE 11

With increasing business variability in mind, the work environment will be constantly monitored to identify opportunities to outsource routine activities to best-of-breed vendors.

Rationale

Outdated assumptions about an enterprise's fixed and variable cost structures are being tested. Businesses are beginning to forgo size in favor of establishing a more "variable" business enterprise—one that can scale to size and capacity as needed. Outsourcing routine activities to best-of-breed vendors is a way of moving an organization toward a more variable cost structure while enhancing the flexibility needed for quick response to evolving customer needs and overall market demands.

Implications

- Organizations must take the time to distinguish between the activities that are core to the operation and essential elements of the business from those activities that are routine and can be effectively outsourced.
- Core business processes that remain internally must be redefined in order to accommodate the outsourcing model being used.
- A process for identifying the best-of-breed vendors from which to consider acquiring outsourcing services is essential.
- New vendor contracting relationships must be established to allow cost-effective outsourcing.
- The act of outsourcing routine activities to outside entities must be developed in such a way as to ensure no disruption to the business.
- Management and staff must be trained in the art of effective outsourcing so that they can be fully aware of the issues and implications underpinning the process.

PRINCIPLE 12

The organization will seek to establish new types of vendor relationships that clearly define mutual gain for the parties involved.

Rationale

The game has changed. The days of the self-sufficient and self-sustaining organization are long gone. The global marketplace requires businesses to establish highly integrated and cooperative relationships with one another. It rewards speed and flexibility.

Consequently, new intercompany relationships continue to be established in order to help firms respond to changes in their respective markets. Ideas such as providing outstanding service and discounted pricing in exchange for a willingness to act as a vendor's showcase account and bartering services in lieu of fees represent just the tip of the iceberg when it comes to developing new and innovative business relationships.

Implications

- Time must be taken to identify mutually beneficial relationships that can contribute to profitable growth of the parties involved.
- Management will have to work with the entire business community to establish new contracting vehicles that provide ways of creating new vendor relationships.
- Existing contracting rules may need to be retired and/or embellished and new rules created in order to better support the establishment of these new vendor relationships.
- Staff will need to be trained in contract administration in order to better manage vendors as they provide specialized services to the organization through these new arrangements.
- Management must be prepared to explore new ways of defining the company's relationships with its providers and continue to be keenly aware of new opportunities of leveraging existing vendor relationships on which the *Best Practices Enterprise*™ relies.

PRINCIPLE 13

The *Best Practices Enterprise*™ will adopt "continuous employee improvement" behaviors.

Rationale

Continuous employee improvement is about placing value on doing things right. It is about creating a work environment where staff members continually expand their capacity to create the results that are truly desired, where new and unrestrained patterns of working are fostered, and where personnel are continually challenged to grow and adjust behavior and performance.

The *Best Practices Enterprise*™ must incorporate continuous employee improvement into the corporate culture in order to meet the competitive challenges of the 21st century. This newly revitalized organization represents a great departure from the current culture at the company. However, it can be established through hard work and perseverance.

Implications

- Staff must become familiar with the characteristics of the continuous employee improvement process. Specialized seminars and training programs should be developed that enable job-related, as well as interpersonal, growth of individual knowledge and skills.

- A learning process must be initiated that reaches every staff member and provides him or her with the opportunity to learn and develop the attitudes, values, and skills needed by the new organization.
- Management must create an environment where it is safe to challenge the *status quo* and must encourage those who are proactively seeking to make changes for the good of the company.
- Leaders, at all levels of the organization, must become responsible for building a business where staff members continually expand their capabilities to understand complexity, clarify vision, and challenge *shared mental models* (i.e., redefining deeply ingrained assumptions about how things *should* be done).
- An environment must be created where calculated risk-taking is encouraged and where mistakes are viewed as learning opportunities.

PRINCIPLE 14

Performance measurement programs will focus on results and not effort.

Rationale

Desired results come with rewarding desired behavior. When performance measurement programs are properly aligned with an organization's mission and strategic vision, preferred outcomes are achieved.

Accordingly, it is important for the *Best Practices Enterprise*™ to measure and reward its personnel based on their contribution to the achievement of desired results and not on their individual effort. While it is true that the act of working hard may, at times, warrant recognition, hard work alone does not deliver the results required within today's highly competitive landscape.

Performance measurement and reward systems must be recalibrated to track results and compensate performance.

Implications

- Current measurement practices must be identified and reviewed for improvement.
- The organization should introduce new performance measurements that map directly to the company's vision.
- Existing measurement programs that do not map directly to the organization's desired outcomes must be retired.
- The management team should be prepared to engage staff in the measurement definition process because frontline employees understand which activities provide value toward achieving business goals.

- An awareness program aimed at educating all employees in the company's mission and strategic vision is important (i.e., otherwise, when engaged in defining appropriate measurements, staff may recommend the measurement of activities that do not directly contribute to the vision).
- Any measurement program should ensure that any variable elements of employee compensation packages are directly tied to performance, with rewards commensurate with contribution.

PRINCIPLE 15

A team-based management model will be adopted by the company to enhance the ability to better respond to emerging market opportunities.

Rationale

The corporate bureaucracy that has held strong for more than a century is gone. Organizations can no longer afford to be top-heavy. More importantly, firms cannot tolerate the lethargy that is present in extensive management bureaucracies. A team-based management model that empowers staff to make procedural adjustments, as needed, in response to market demands must replace the aged chain-of-command approach that has been around since the early Industrial Age.

Implications

- Personnel at all levels of the company must be trained in the rudiments of team-based management.
- The organization must reexamine its existing reporting structure and identify ways in which to break it down in order to introduce a team-based management model.
- Related performance measurement, personnel administration, and other human resource management procedures must be adjusted to accommodate the new team-based approaches under consideration.
- The management team must make certain that proper measures are instituted to ensure that necessary controls are maintained and that appropriate business practices and decorum continue to be followed.

WITH THAT SAID

These 15 business principles provide a solid context for understanding the best practices programs that are discussed in detail in the next several chapters. Practitioners and their managers, who may be charged with overseeing the implementation of specific best practices, may want to pay particular attention to these chapters because they provide excellent guidance on the *wherefores* and the *whys* of each program.

With the business principles as a backdrop, let us now examine "program-centric strategic planning," the first of the best practices.

* * *

3

PROGRAM-CENTRIC STRATEGIC PLANNING

*The inner workings of **Your Company, Inc.** have changed as well. Strategic planning has been institutionalized. It is an ongoing process that keeps track of all of the activities going on within the company.*

The world's "interconnectedness" has made access to people and information as easy as a mouse click. The emergence and maturation of the Internet have provided immense opportunities to tie businesses together and have allowed firms to gain exposure to customers and markets that they could have only dreamed about penetrating in the past.

Couple this phenomenon with the emergence of the "pay as you go" attitude that many *Best Practices Enterprises*™ are adopting through outsourcing models that redefine assumptions about fixed and variable cost structures and capital investments, and one can see that a different way of strategic thinking and planning is needed for ongoing success in the 21st century.

Put simply, most organizations are ill-prepared for the competitive demands that lie ahead, and they lack the discipline and rigor needed to identify, organize, and execute the appropriate work in any sustainable way. Without an advanced way of planning and orchestrating strategic direction-setting, firms will continue to flounder in the new age. For this reason, *Program-Centric Strategic Planning* is the first best practices program that we will examine (see Figure 3.1). It sets the stage for the other best practices programs that follow later in the book.

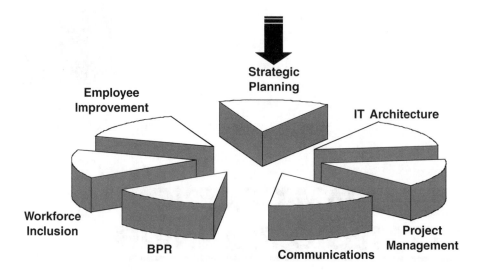

Figure 3.1   Strategic planning is the first piece of the puzzle.

WHY "MORE OF THE SAME" WILL NOT CUT IT

Strategic planning is one of those things that every company claims to do, but few strategic plans ever seem to become more than dust-ridden "shelfware" used to shimmy a door open every now and again.

In practice most firms view strategic planning as an annual event tied to the budget cycle. Each year, the department heads go through this painful process of "roughing-out" their basic ideas of what their business areas will be doing during the following year. Once determined, they begin to estimate (in round numbers) how much all that work will cost. These estimates are gathered together by the Comptroller or Chief Financial Officer, and the departmental budgets are doled out.

That is all well and good; however, annual budget-setting is not strategic planning. Rather, strategic planning is an ongoing, continuous process used to identify, document, and oversee all the strategic, tactical, and operational-related initiatives under way (and intended to be done) within an enterprise.

The best strategic plans are program-centric. Program-centric strategic planning is an essential element of a *Best Practices Enterprise*™.

WHAT IS PROGRAM-CENTRIC STRATEGIC PLANNING?

Program-centric strategic plans organize initiatives into projects and programs. Projects are initiatives that are performed once and are done. Programs are initiatives that are ongoing by nature and will continue into the future. Programs can spawn one or more projects and/or programs (depending on the needs of the organization).

Here are some examples of the types of initiatives that may constitute a program-centric strategic plan:

- Strategic acquisitions program
- Results-focused communications program
- Uninterrupted business redesign program
- Continuous employee improvement program
- Cross-cultural workforce inclusion program
- Shop floor safety program
- Resilient systems design project
- Corporate branding project
- Product evaluation project
- Union issues awareness project
- CIO search/selection project
- Sarbanes–Oxley prep project

The content of a program-centric strategic plan ranges from the heady (strategic acquisition program) to the commonplace (CIO search/selection project). Regardless, it is essential that the plan encompasses all the strategic, tactical, and operational-related efforts to be performed within the enterprise. If it does that, the plan will accurately reflect the firm's strategic direction.

A program-centric strategic plan, one that truly reveals the firm's strategic direction, is perhaps the most important management tool that an organization can have at its disposal because it is a roadmap into its future. It outlines the specific projects and programs needed for evolving the concern into a *Best Practices* business. Indeed, once established, the program-centric strategic plan holds the "formula" for success in the new millennium.

As outlined in Chapter 1, businesses are heading into a time when they will be in a continual state of transformation. The business environment will force firms to move faster than ever before. Organizations will need a strategic plan that allows for rapid and dynamic change. Program-centric plans can deliver this flexibility as long as the company using the technique keeps the plans up-to-date.

STAYING CURRENT

In order to ensure that the program-centric strategic plan always reflects the current state of affairs within the enterprise, firms must establish a robust program-centric strategic planning program that transforms the usual, annual planning activities into a set of full-time, continuous practices. In this way, the program-centric strategic plan that results will act as an anchor point for the organization to gauge its strategic direction. Business leadership and staff alike can use such a plan as a common reference source to judge the merits of new ideas and to determine their appropriate "fit" within the company dynamic.

Indeed, organizations can no longer afford to view strategic plans as simply placeholders for last year's ideas about the future. Program-centric strategic plans must echo what is happening inside the company right now. If they do anything less, then the plan is not worth much more than the dusty doorstop referenced earlier.

So what should a program-centric strategic planning program look like in order to deliver the value needed by businesses to be successful in years to come?

THE PERFECT PROGRAM

Most contemporary strategic plans contain a bit of visioning, a dash of goal setting, and a whole lot of budget estimating. But the contents of a program-centric strategic plan really should not be limited to just these. All kinds of initiatives, from building computer systems to acquiring new companies, can constitute a program-centric strategic plan. A plan's content is dependent on where a firm is today and where it wants to be in the future.

A program-centric strategic plan should be thought of as a master blueprint that contains the entire listing of the projects and programs needed by the organization. Yes, a target vision and goals for the business are important strategic elements of a solid program-centric strategic plan. However, the projects and programs that a firm pursues are where the work is done. These must be constantly monitored and refined for an organization to successfully maneuver from its starting point (where it is today) to its destination (where it wants to be tomorrow).

With that said, a solid program-centric strategic planning program can be characterized as providing the enterprise with:

- A mechanism(s) for identifying new project ideas and proposing initiatives that all stakeholders of the business (e.g., employee, customer, supplier, stockholder) can easily understand and use
- A standard process for developing project plans for these proposed initiatives that defines such details as goals, objectives, success factors, staffing needs, and task lists
- A means of setting new, and reestablishing existing, business priorities based on the standard, proposed project plans that optimize the leveraging of company assets to competitive gain

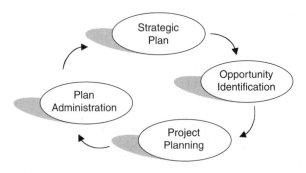

Figure 3.2 A simplified program-centric strategic planning framework.

- A definition of the resources and methods needed to build and administer the program-centric strategic plan as it evolves over time

The program-centric strategic planning process that encompasses these attributes does not have to be complicated. In fact, the simpler the process, the better it is. Staff members are more likely to follow a process that is simple to apply and delivers the desired results.

The diagram presented in Figure 3.2 is from a Fortune 500 firm that I have worked with over the years. It illustrates how straightforward a program-centric strategic planning framework can be.

Note that there are only four steps in the process. In the first step, new opportunities are identified and presented to an executive steering committee. The committee is made up of the senior management team from across the organization. It has been put into place for the express purpose of defining priorities and redeploying resources as required in meeting the strategic needs of the firm.

To make the job of priority-setting easier, a firm should document new project opportunities in a consistent way. A project opportunities template can be crafted and used to capture the name, description, objectives, criticality, size, risks, and interdependences related to each new idea being put forth. (Refer to Appendix A for examples of how each *Best Practices* initiatives would be documented using a project opportunities template.)

Once a proposed project is approved by the committee, a project champion is named, a team is established, and a detailed project plan is built. The project plan should extend the information presented in the project opportunities template in order to provide all the details that a project manager will need to manage the effort. Additional information to be provided in the project plan includes:

- Objectives
- Enablers

- Constraints
- Task lists
- Delivery schedules
- Critical success factors
- Special skills/tools required
- Completion criteria

The completed plan is then provided to the strategic planning administrators, who add it to the firm's program-centric strategic plan. The new edition of the program-centric strategic plan is then published and distributed across the firm.

Some of the benefits of this kind of program-centric strategic planning process include:

- *Inclusion*—It encourages everyone in the company to contribute ideas for new initiatives through the opportunity identification step.
- *Discipline*—Because of the project planning emphasis built into the approach, all work is done in the company in a deliberate and programmed way.
- *Executive participation*—The typical parochialism found in many firms' planning practices is diminished because the senior executives are brought together at the same planning table, providing a simple way for them to keep each other honest.
- *Full-time emphasis*—The program-centric strategic plan administrators are responsible for overseeing the publication and distribution of the plan. They also track all of the projects under way within the company and provide periodic status reports to the senior committee. This helps management to better understand which projects are on-time and on-budget and which ones need some help or should be considered for elimination altogether—making room for new project opportunities that may better deliver the desired results to the enterprise.

It is easy to recognize that there are many benefits to be derived from putting a solid, yet simple, planning approach in place. It seems that good things begin to happen whenever a current and accessible program-centric strategic planning process becomes a foundation stone for the business—more order and discipline, less chaos and waste (see The Rolls-Royce sidebar for an example of what a company can accomplish through exceptional planning).

Now, let us explore ways in which organizations can kick-start a program-centric strategic planning program.

BEST PRACTICES BUSINESS IN ACTION

Rolls-Royce Aerospace: The Sky Is the Limit

In an effort to improve, Rolls-Royce, plc, a company whose brand represents excellence, teamed with A.T. Kearney and EDS to develop a program-centric business plan within its aerospace division.

The planning effort is organized into six broad areas (or programs), including:

- Repair and overhaul
- Integrated engine program management
- Component production and engine assembly
- Product development and customer support integration
- Strategic sourcing
- Supply chain management

Several of the completed projects have already delivered results. For example, a new repair tracking system has cut overhaul time in half, while enhancing technician productivity by 10%; the supply chain management initiatives resulted in improved business flow management that yielded a doubling of inventory turnover; at the same time, product development and customer support process redesign activities reduced jet engine prototype development time by one third.

Indeed, Rolls-Royce Aerospace is proving that the sky is the limit (pardon the pun) when solid planning practices are institutionalized and the resultant projects and programs that constitute the plan are executed in a timely and deliberate *Best Practices* way.

Source: Based on "Aerospace & Defense Case Studies," www.atkearney.com, 2004.

GETTING STARTED

Establishing a program-centric strategic planning program is an important step toward actualization of a *Best Practices Enterprise*™ for the program-centric strategic plan is the place where all initiatives should be defined and documented. Any type of project or program that a company embarks upon should be reflected in the plan.

The process for establishing a program-centric strategic planning program includes:

- Establishing a project
- Charging a team
- Forming an executive steering committee
- Developing and accepting the planning process recommendation
- Promoting the use of the recommended process

- Forming a program-centric strategic planning administration function
- Providing staff with project planning training.

Let us probe what is involved in each of these steps.

Establishing the Project

Typically, it requires 3 to 6 months of full-time work to institute a program-centric strategic planning program. Companies should view the creation of the program-centric strategic planning program as a project that has a definite beginning, middle, and ending. The scope of the effort is to establish a planning program, not necessarily to build the plan (although the creation of an initial plan can be included too). Once the program is in place, the project is considered complete and the process of program-centric strategic planning is then institutionalized through the execution of the program.

To get started, a project champion should be identified who will be responsible for overseeing the project and ensuring that all is done well. Typically, the project champion is a senior executive involved in direction-setting for the concern. He or she may even be the CEO or company president. However, other members of the executive staff can guide the project, as long as the project champion is well respected by his or her peers.

Charging the Team

Once the champion is identified, he or she should establish a project team and have them begin the work of creating a program-centric strategic planning program for the company. This team will be responsible for defining and documenting the "who, what, where, and how" of the program-centric strategic planning program.

The team should be constituted of staff members who have experience in developing business processes and policies. Members should have extensive project management experience and strong communication skills. They will need to document their recommendations and present them to senior management in a persuasive way.

One of the members should be named as the project leader and be given the responsibility and authority for managing the day-to-day activities of the team. The project leader should have a deep-rooted understanding of what program-centric strategic planning is all about and be able to direct the team to meaningful conclusions regarding how program-centric strategic planning should be done at the company.

Some organizations develop a network of forward-thinking individuals within the firm to act as an advisory council for the program-centric strategic

BEST PRACTICES BUSINESS IN ACTION

The Fast Track Program-Centric Business Planning at Siemens Nixdorf

Siemens Nixdorf Information Systems (SNI), Europe's largest computer company, has taken the idea of a program-centric business planning advisory council to new heights. A few years ago, the firm decided to choose 23 young, fast-track employees from across the company to tutor top management on emerging technologies in hopes that the insight provided would help management identify new markets for the future.

The idea is that these young people are better positioned than the senior management staff to understand new technologies and to recognize emerging trends as they emanate in our society's next generation of consumers.

Through one-on-one interactions with members of the management board, the FutureScape team, as it is called, helps the firm to see long-term social, business, economic, and technological trends and discontinuities that it might otherwise miss.

FutureScape members convene a meeting in their home offices every month to answer questions about the planning process. This helps foster information sharing across the company and gets others involved in the program-centric business planning process. Good ideas are often contributed by people in the field because they have first-hand knowledge of what is really going on in the business. FutureScape members can then bring these ideas forward to the management board so that they can choose to act on them.

Obviously, this advisory council model is working at SNI. Will it, or some variation, work for you and your company? It is certainly a best practices business idea that is worth exploring.

Source: Based on "Strategy is for the Young," by Kate A. Kane, Fast Company, April/May 1996, p. 26.

planning team (see Siemens Nixdorf sidebar). The council augments the team by providing input—helping to extend the team's collective knowledge and establishing a network of planning disciples who will readily understand the process when it is unveiled down the road.

Forming an Executive Steering Committee

With the team in place and working, the project champion should then form an executive steering committee (ESC) to review and improve the team's deliverables. Comprised of senior management, the steering committee has the responsibility to direct the team toward recommendations that they believe are appropriate and practical for the company.

The committee should be chaired by the highest ranking senior executive, usually the president or CEO of the organization. This level of participation shows the team and company staff that senior management is committed to improving the way it does program-centric strategic planning.

The steering committee will be briefed by the team on a monthly basis throughout the project. By frequently reviewing interim progress, the senior staff is ensured that the team's final product will be both sound and sufficiently detailed to be implemented by the organization.

Once established, the steering committee becomes a very important cog in the firm's direction-setting machinery. It will remain in place forever and serve as a governing body for all things strategic within the company. We will see in later chapters just how important an ESC is to a firm preparing for great change.

Devising and Accepting a Planning Process Recommendation

Regardless of the specifics, a program-centric strategic plan should always reflect where an organization is heading in the future and contain the individual project/program plans for the firm's current and ongoing efforts.

With that said, the project team's planning process recommendation must have certain characteristics to be considered viable. For example, it should specify a method for developing the initial program-centric strategic plan, contain a procedure for identifying new project/program opportunities, and establish a mechanism that ensures that the program-centric strategic plan evolves over time.

The recommendation should also answer such basic questions as:

- Who will develop the initial plan?
- What will it look like?
- How will the plan be developed?
- When will it be delivered?
- Who will maintain the plan once it is delivered?
- When will it be updated?
- How will updates be distributed?

With these details captured, the ESC should have little trouble reviewing and refining the recommendation. Once refined, the ESC can begin to help promote the use of the proposed program-centric strategic planning program.

Promoting the Use of the Recommended Planning Process

Once the recommendation has been refined and accepted by the ESC, the next step is to begin to promote its use within the firm. This can take many forms and is usually some combination of:

- A formal executive announcement declaring that the firm has established a new planning process

- The publication of program-centric strategic planning program recommendations and deliverables (as developed by the project team)
- The creation of an awareness program that aims to educate employees in the planning process and their role in it

This kind of activity goes a long way in solidifying the importance of program-centric strategic planning in the organization. But perhaps the most important aspect of promotion is adherence to the process itself by the senior staff.

Employees often discount what their managers are espousing at any point in time. Most of us have seen new management ideas come and go. But everyone pays attention to what their managers are doing. If executives skirt the process and find loopholes that allow them to get their particular agendas met in spite of the program-centric strategic planning process, then employees will not follow the process either. However, if the executives are living by the plan and following the rules of the process, then the workers will play their role in it as well.

Forming a Strategic Planning Office Function

The formation of a strategic planning office (SPO) is an important part of strengthening the program-centric strategic planning program within a company. Staffing a full-time position or positions to oversee the planning process sends a message to employees that planning is an important priority for the firm.

The basic responsibilities of the SPO include:

- Conducting monthly project coordination meetings
- Conducting quarterly ESC meetings
- Updating and publishing the strategic plan
- Communicating strategic plan changes to the stakeholder community
- Reviewing the status of projects/programs presented in the plan
- Facilitating cross-project sharing of information/solutions
- Identifying opportunities to consolidate strategic efforts
- Assisting project managers in adjusting their project plans

Needless to say, the planning function positions must be staffed by competent and respected people. There is sometimes a tendency to place "cast-off" employees in new planning positions. Doing this sends the organization down a slippery slope to failure. The management team must place individuals who know the business, know the industry, possess strong communication skills, and are business savvy—all essential attributes for getting the job done.

Positioning the Strategic Planning Office within the Organization

Once the talent is secured, the management team must tackle the placement of the function within the company. Often, the strategic planning function reports to the CEO. A better option is the appointment of a chief planning officer (CPO) to oversee the function. By making such an appointment, *Best Practices Enterprises*™ are making a bold statement about the importance of program-centric strategic planning.

Interestingly, some firms even have the planning function reporting to the ESC. However, this can become problematic, with *no one* responsible party to look after the staff. For this kind of reporting structure to work, the planners will need the ESC to continually give them strong direction, otherwise, the planning function may lose its bearings (see Trouble On High sidebar for more insight).

Providing Staff with Project Planning Training

A key aspect of the planning process is the development of the individual project and program plans that together make up the organization's program-centric strategic plan. Personnel should be provided project planning training so that they are better prepared to develop and plan the initiatives that will move the firm forward.

The training does not have to be elaborate to be effective. It should focus on the fundamentals of sound planning. A focus on proper staffing, task estimation, and time-line development is all that is needed to get the foundation established. Once founded, more sophisticated training modules can be added as needed.

ESC members should be included in the first wave of people going through the training. It is important for them to fully understand the dynamics of project planning so that they can better understand the underpinnings of the program-centric strategic plan that they are driving.

We should not assume that the management team naturally knows about project planning and management just because they are senior leaders. If necessary, an executive training component should be established just for the senior management team. Remember, many executives earned their stripes long before the popularization of the concept of project planning and management.

AS AN ASIDE

It was pointed out earlier in the chapter that the project team charged with developing the program-centric strategic planning program may not necessarily be responsible for creating the organization's initial program-centric strategic plan.

BEST PRACTICES BUSINESS IN ACTION
Trouble on High

A manufacturing industry client had put a program-centric strategic planning process in place a year or two before I began working with them. The management there had done many of the right things in getting the planning program off the ground. But management was not satisfied that the program-centric strategic planning process was where it really needed to be.

The steering committee that was formed was not functioning properly. It seemed that many of the projects and programs that made up the firm's strategic plan were really aimed at serving specific parochial interests and were not directed toward the greatest good of the company. There was fear that assets were being squandered on initiatives that were not going to provide the benefits that were promised.

What I found as I began my investigation into the problem was that the three-person planning group (created early in the program-centric strategic planning program) was reporting directly to the ESC. This meant that none of the executives at the planning table had direct responsibility for the plan or the planners.

Consequently, the executives gave the planning process lip service—and went about doing their own thing within their respective areas using whatever budget dollars were allocated to them. The planners struck a reactive stance (rather than a proactive one) to the goings on within the company and began to merely document the projects and programs under way and to place the write-ups in the strategic plan.

Under this model, the ESC was never given an opportunity to steer. The committee meetings became a form of glorified status reporting, where each executive simply discussed what he or she was doing. The management team never collectively engaged in a business strategy or direction-setting discussion.

We fixed the problem. The planning group became part of strategic acquisitions and business development and began reporting to that area's group vice president. Soon after shifting the reporting lines, the face of program-centric strategic planning at the company changed. Almost suddenly it seemed that the planning process began to be enforced and the executives who were accustomed to doing what they pleased with their budget dollars were brought under scrutiny. In essence, the spigot was turned off. Program-centric strategic planning was now a senior executive's priority.

It should be pointed out that the company's original reporting model does have its merits. It provides a level of objectivity that might be difficult to attain in a different reporting structure. However, this organization was suffering because its culture was based on a command-and-control model that required senior executive ownership to function. Once we addressed this subtlety, everything fell into place for the company's planning process. It began to work the way a *Best Practices Enterprise*™ should.

But, an initial program-centric strategic plan does need to be built. So who does it?

If one does not exist, the program-centric strategic planning staff will spearhead the initial program-centric strategic plan development effort. In fact, the development of the initial plan may be the planning function's first project.

In order to get it off the ground, the planners will need to first spend time with each of the ESC members. This will help the planners get the "lay of the land" and better understand what each of the senior executives believes are the most important issues and priorities for the enterprise.

As the interviews are taking place, an inventory of the projects and programs that are currently under way (or planned for the future) should also be taken. This will help establish a baseline. This baseline of current projects and programs will be the start of the initial program-centric strategic plan. The baseline will then be adjusted and augmented as needed to address the issues discovered through the executive interview cycle.

New projects and programs will be added to the baseline. Some of the efforts under way, or currently planned for, may take a back seat as a result. Once the adjustments are complete, the planners will have created a short list, in effect, of the initiatives that they believe should be pursued by the firm.

Using an opportunity planning template, like those found in Appendix A, the planners set about documenting each of the initiatives on the list—forming the initial program-centric strategic plan. When complete, the ESC is convened to review the plan, and refinements are made. Once the executives sign off on the initial plan, it is published and dispersed throughout the organization. Project managers are assigned to each of the initiatives, and detailed project and program plans are developed—then it is off to the races!

It should be noted that some firms (see 3M sidebar for an example) also include written mission statements, strategic visions, and alternative scenario discussions in the plan. This helps company staff members to better understand the context of the projects and programs that make up the program-centric strategic plan. It also serves as a backdrop for some of the strategic choices that will need to be made in the future—giving the firm a step up over the competition.

Such additions to a plan are like the icing on a cake and should be developed as the firm's overall program-centric strategic planning matures over time.

IN CLOSING

The kind of program-centric strategic planning approach presented here, one that focuses on projects and programs and not just on the budget, provides decision-makers with information about what is going on behind the battle lines where the war is fought every day.

BEST PRACTICES BUSINESS IN ACTION

3M's Planning Story

A few years ago, 3M was having trouble getting its people to really understand and buy into the company's business direction. Gordon Shaw, who oversaw strategic planning at 3M at the time, was troubled by this. So, he introduced strategic narratives to the firm's program-centric strategic planning process as a means to address this issue.

Strategic narratives take the form of a story. They explain the current situation, the market, the economy, and the players in the industry. A good narrative includes details about the obstacles and hazards that the company must face when pursuing the plan and discusses the ways for overcoming these challenges and succeeding in achieving the company's goals and objectives.

It was Shaw's belief that this format was far more compelling than the traditional bullet lists that were used by the firm in years past. As a by-product, strategic narratives force their authors to really think out their business strategies and to try to engage support from co-workers for the projects and programs being positioned—resulting in better program-centric plans and strategies for 3M.

The approach is already paying dividends for the company. A strategic narrative was used to pitch the notion of establishing a joint venture with Hoechst AG (a German chemical company). The narrative must have been very impressive to have been approved. At 3M, international joint ventures are not a generally popular proposition.

As a result a new $350 million business was born.

Source: Based on "Strategic stories: how 3M is rewriting business planning," by Gordon Shaw, Robert Brown, and Philip Bromiley, *Harvard Business Review*, May–June 1998, pp. 41–50.

This insight is essential to running a successful enterprise in the global marketplace that is upon us. It is the difference between order and chaos—winning and losing. All firms interested in being optimally positioned for the future should follow suit and adopt a simple program-centric strategic planning model that is easy to understand and use.

Program-centric strategic planning is a *Best Practices Enterprise*™ fundamental. Let us look at how systems-related planning fits into the model for success in the new era.

* * *

Web
Added
Value™

This book has free material available from download from the
Web Added Value™ resource center at *www.jrosspub.com*

SAMPLE OPPORTUNITIES IDENTIFICATION DOCUMENTS (THE BEST PRACTICES)

THE TEMPLATE HELPS STANDARDIZE PROGRAM DESCRIPTIONS

Each initiative described in the standard opportunity identification template includes:

- Name
- Description
- Objectives
- Criticality
- Size
- Risks
- Interdependencies

In this way, project/program descriptions are standardized and the reader can quickly grasp the intention of each potential initiative—enhancing the company's understanding of the importance of an opportunity.

PROGRAMS COVERED IN THE DOCUMENT

The programs covered in this document include all of the *Best Practices* programs that are needed to keep the company competitive well into the future. The programs include:

- Program-centric strategic planning
- Resilient IT architecture (RITA) design
- Results-focused communications
- Portfolio-based project management
- Uninterrupted business redesign (U-BPR)
- Cross-functional workforce inclusion
- Continuous employee improvement

Below are completed samples of each opportunities identification template.

Program-Centric Strategic Planning Program

This project focuses on establishing a strategic planning program that organizes initiatives into projects and programs. *Projects* are initiatives that are performed once and are finished. *Programs* are initiatives that are ongoing by nature and that will continue into the future. Programs can spawn one or more projects and/or programs (depending on the needs of the organization). It is essential that the plan encompasses all the strategic, tactical, and operational-related efforts to be performed within the enterprise.

Together with the senior management team, the project team will develop the initial program-centric strategic plan. Once completed, an administrative process will be defined and implemented to ensure that the strategic planning process remains ongoing.

Objectives

- To develop a program-centric strategic plan for XYZ Insurance Corporation (XYZ) that defines all the projects and programs required to support the achievement of the firm's strategic objectives
- To determine the planning administration process requirements needed to maintain and modify the plan over time
- To establish an ongoing strategic planning process

Criticality

High

Size

Medium

Risks

If the project is not done:
> The firm will continue to suffer from all of the ills associated with poor planning, including increased cost of operations, inability to respond quickly to emerging market opportunities, and an unstable work environment.

If the project is put in place:
> Company politics may be allowed to creep into the prioritization process, short-circuiting the entire planning effort.

Interdependencies

None identified

RESILIENT IT ARCHITECTURE DESIGN PROGRAM

This project focuses on establishing an IT architecture design that will create the technology environment needed to support the mission of the entire enterprise. It is essential that the resultant architecture has systems resiliency built in.

The project is made up of distinct phases. Each phase will produce specific deliverables. Together, these deliverables will constitute the resilient IT architecture (RITA) for the company.

Once completed, an ongoing architecture administration process will be defined and implemented to ensure that the architecture always supports the firm's stated business direction.

Objectives

- To develop a RITA design for XYZ that defines all the technology-related projects and programs required to support the achievement of the firm's strategic objectives
- To determine the IT architecture administration process requirements needed to maintain and modify the architecture over time
- To establish an ongoing architecture administration process

Criticality

High

Size

Medium

Risks

If the project is not done:
> Manual operations will continue to be the norm through much of the enterprise. Service credibility will be threatened if inadequate systems are allowed to prevail. A wide range of threats, including natural disasters, terrorism, and human error, can cripple the current IT environment without the proper safeguards being designed-in to the IT architecture.

If the project is put in place:
> Time must be dedicated to the consideration of systems extensibility, application portability, and interoperability to ensure rapid redeployment capabilities and the resiliency of the architecture.

Interdependencies

Data management issues surrounding "ownership" of the data will become an issue over time. A corporate policy on the subject must be defined.

RESULTS-FOCUSED COMMUNICATION PROGRAM

The company's communication program will be an ongoing effort that is intended to oversee the process of effectively and efficiently communicating information to the company staff and other important stakeholders, both inside and outside the company.

The program will be made up of three basic components, including:

- Internal communications project
- External communications project
- Headquarters communications project

These efforts will likely adopt a cross-functional approach to the corporate communications challenge—with all the company's organizational units and departments being pulled into the efforts once they are under way.

The program will work to leverage existing communication devices such as:

- Company newsletter
- Teleconferences
- TV monitors
- Operating committee meetings
- Project coordination meetings
- Departmental staff meetings
- Newsletters

- Company intranet
- e-mail bulletin boards
- Guest presentations
- "Road show" briefings
- Quality reviews

It will also identify new ways of affecting the type of communication processes desired by all stakeholders of the firm.

Objectives

- To develop a communication strategy that defines what, when, where, how, and why information is disseminated throughout the enterprise
- To improve business outcomes by improving the flow of information throughout the company
- To oversee the establishment, use, and evolution of the company's business communications infrastructure
- To improve the company home office communications through its business units
- To proactively and creatively utilize communication to educate the company's customers and producers
- To improve the company's corporate image by providing better information to all stakeholders

Criticality

High

Size

Medium

Risks

If the project is not done:

Uncertainty will continue to distract personnel from performing their core activities. Rumors and mixed messages will exist and informal communication channels will perpetuate. Morale will be negatively affected.

If the project is put in place:

Creditability will be threatened if mixed messages or lack of follow-through emerges.

Interdependencies

Planning committee endorsement

PORTFOLIO-BASED PROJECT MANAGEMENT PROGRAM

The company has a multitude of projects and programs to implement, including those that are yet to be identified within the other best practices programs discussed in this document. Clearly, a consistent and efficient project management methodology should be put in place to assist in their delivery. The goal of this program is to institute such a methodology and to instill a "project management mentality" within the company culture.

This initiative will be incorporated into the daily work setting. It will promote the notion of managing all of these stated initiatives as a portfolio of projects and programs necessary to drive the business closer to the achievement of its vision. It will develop the project management approach that the company will adopt for all its project/programs. Likely, a training course aimed at management and staff alike will be driven out of this program as a way to *jump start* the initiative.

Objectives

- To develop and adopt a company project management methodology
- To introduce the benefits of project management to the company
- To foster a "project management" mentality throughout the organization
- To improve the company's ability to manage work activities by instituting a portfolio management process for maintaining all of the firm's projects and programs
- To train personnel on the firm's project management methodology and the techniques needed to ensure the successful implementation of project/programs

Criticality

High

Size

Medium

Risks

If the project is not done:
Inconsistent project management (PM) approaches will waste resources. As additional projects and programs are identified and funded, they may continue to stall and fail.

If the project is put in place:

Simple and straightforward PM elements must first be identified and instituted. With momentum, more sophisticated PM practices can then be introduced.

Interdependencies

- Strategic planning process
- Continuous employee improvement program
- Formalized project management office (PMO) process

UNINTERRUPTED BUSINESS REDESIGN PROGRAM

The overarching theme of this program is to institutionalize a process of continually optimizing the business. The process chosen to do this must be characterized by:

- Planning (what to do)
- Doing (what is planned)
- Checking (the results of what is done against the plan)
- Acting (by updating the plan for the next time the work is to be performed)

By doing so, improvement activities can be monitored to determine whether the results match projected benefits. If envisioned benefits are not being delivered, adjustments are planned and executed.

The planning of this program will focus on how the dimensions of people, processes, and technology can be improved to better align activities with the corporate vision.

Once a methodology is selected and appropriate training is delivered, all of the firm's departments will be called upon to begin the uninterrupted business redesign program (U-BPR) activities. Indeed, it is likely that this program will spawn the following programs that will all share the methodology as an underpinning:

- Underwriting improvement
- Accounting and finance improvement
- Statistical reporting improvement
- Government affairs improvement
- Human resources improvement
- Loss control improvement
- Marketing improvement

- Claims improvement
- Information systems improvement

Objectives

- To institutionalize continuous improvement techniques in the company as a means of improving its business operation
- To ensure that the company management and staff continuously work to improve all that the company does
- To create a culture that promotes active self-examination of work plans, activities, procedures, and measurements
- To establish a responsive, flexible, and repeatable business reengineering process that can be used throughout the organization
- To identify a project-based pathway for guiding the organization toward a more efficient and successful future

Criticality

High

Size

Large

Risks

If the project is not done:
A misalignment of resources may result throughout the organization, causing unnecessary expenditures. Delivery services may be inconsistent and inefficient throughout the enterprise. Staff may continue to feel that change is not possible.

If the project is put in place:
Care must be taken to ensure that "the business of the company" does not suffer as the firm pursues improvement ideas.

Interdependencies

A solid business redesign methodology must be adopted and used, and ongoing funding may be an issue.

CROSS-CULTURAL WORKFORCE INCLUSION PROGRAM

This program is an ongoing effort to advance the thinking related to leveraging the differences that exist among personnel as a means of gaining a competitive edge in the marketplace. By rethinking existing cultural paradigms and recasting them in ways that will help the organization benefit from individual differences that exist in the workforce, XYZ will be best positioned to address the challenges awaiting it in this new age of business globalization.

Objectives

- To enhance workforce quality by creating a highly attractive work setting
- To improve performance by fostering inclusion and providing opportunities for staff to be heard and valued
- To gain access to new markets by better using the diverse workforce to introduce it to a broader customer base
- To enhance decision-making by promoting new ways of thinking and doing
- To create a better corporate culture by introducing a higher level of energy and originality into the workplace

Criticality

High

Size

Medium

Risks

If the project is not put in place:
The firm runs the risk of languishing within its existing corporate culture because it fails to best leverage the differences that exist within its workforce. Competitors can pull ahead if they recognize the value of diversity and inclusion and begin efforts to use their diversity more strategically.

If the project is put in place:
The firm must be careful not to allow the program to become a source of reverse discrimination. The firm must be sure to educate and raise proper awareness so that the program is not misconstrued as just another EEO initiative.

Interdependencies

Continuous employee improvement program

CONTINUOUS EMPLOYEE IMPROVEMENT PROGRAM

The continuous employee improvement program is made up of two major elements—performance measurement and training and education. The performance measurement component aims to ensure that the company develops appropriate performance measurements, aligns them with its corporate vision, and integrates them into the employee performance evaluation process.

This piece of the program will be driven by company senior management and department heads. These individuals, as the company's management team, will be responsible for ensuring that the initial set of performance measurements is appropriately defined and used.

By tying the employee performance evaluation process to the company performance measurement program, the management team will improve its ability to motivate employees to do what must be done to best achieve the company's mission. In time, the program will ensure that the systems supporting core business processes will be designed to capture key performance metrics (i.e., productivity measurements) as a by-product of executing work activities and also become a valuable delivery system for required training.

The training and education element of the continuous employee improvement program, on the other hand, ensures that company management and staff are provided with appropriate opportunities to develop the skills required to help the company achieve its goals and objectives.

The program will be responsible for developing the curriculum for each training course offered within the company. It will determine such details as:

- Training mode (e.g., on-the-job, self-study, classroom)
- Training media (instructor-led, study guides, videos, etc.)
- Target training audience
- Course sequence and schedule

OBJECTIVES

- To align measurements with the company's vision statement, business goals, and objectives
- To improve business results by introducing appropriate work measurements
- To integrate the measurement program with the employee performance evaluation process
- To motivate staff to change behaviors accordingly to enhance their ability to meet expected results
- To identify the necessary components of a comprehensive training and education program

- To ensure appropriate linkages between the program and the strategic direction of the company
- To establish a plan for implementing the training and education program within the company
- To further the firm's desire to establish a "learning organization"

Criticality

High

Size

Large

Risks

If the project is not done:

Staff will continue to work at cross purposes, uncertain as to which activities are important. Inefficiencies will persist and work quality will suffer. Training will remain informal and ineffective.

If the project is put in place:

Care must be taken to identify appropriate measurements and monitoring activities. Time should be taken to design performance measurement processes that can be automated as systems mature within the company. Poorly planned or timed training will negatively impact core activities and waste resources.

Interdependences

Technology support and maturity

IN CLOSING

This document presents a set of proposed projects and programs that the strategic planning project team believes is essential to achieving the company's vision for the future. It should be noted that all of these anticipated initiatives share a common trait—their successful implementation is dependent on the company management team's willingness to staff, fund, and support them. Without clear management commitment, all these efforts will likely *fall flat.*

* * *

RESILIENT IT ARCHITECTURE DESIGN

The use of automation to compete has matured immensely. **Your Business, Inc.** *has formalized, and aggressively manages, an information systems architecture. The architecture provides a blueprint for the types of information, systems, and technologies needed to support the business.*

The philosophy of the *Best Practices Enterprise*™ requires that organizations learn to respond quickly to changes in the marketplace and streamline operations so that workflow changes can be made "on the fly." Businesses can no longer expect that their customers will be willing to wait for them. Rather, consumers and trading partners alike are ready and able to move on if their needs are not met expeditiously.

This puts tremendous pressure on firms to fully automate business operations—designing systems in such a way that the underlying business processes and workflows can be adjusted dynamically without any business disruption.

The fact that companies are doing business from the far corners of the globe introduces additional challenges as well. Automated applications, as such, must be designed to be highly durable and able to be instantly reconfigured as business needs dictate.

For instance, imagine that an earthquake has struck the San Fernando Valley and your firm's West Coast operations computing capabilities are wiped out. What do you do? With a resilient IT architecture (RITA) in place, a firm can

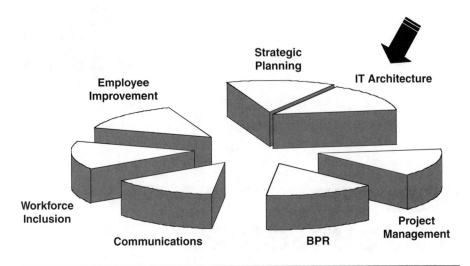

Figure 4.1 IT architecture is the next practice to add.

reroute its processing capabilities to its Boston branch and it will not "miss a beat."

Obviously, the ability to respond in this way is no accident. Work must be done to design a solid IT environment that can handle the situation. Clearly, information technology deployment must be more than simply *planned and designed well*. It must be "architected" for flexibility and resilience. RITA *design* is the next business fundamental to examine in our best practices exploration. It is the second piece of the pie as depicted in Figure 4.1.

WHAT IS RESILIENT IT ARCHITECTURE?

In order to get a full understanding of RITA, we must dissect the terms. Let us start with the word "architecture." What do you think of when you read the word architecture? Most of us think of a house, or a church, or some ruins in Rome.

Webster's II New Riverside University Dictionary defines architecture this way:

> ar•chi•tec•ture n. 1. The art and science of designing and erecting buildings. 2. Architectural structures as a whole. 3. A style and method of design and construction <Roman *Architecture*>. 4. Design or system perceived by humans <the architecture of the solar system>.

Clearly, one does not usually associate information systems or computer technology with architecture. Let us change that to enhance our understanding of RITA.

Building Construction	Information Systems
Site Plan	Operations Plan
Floor Plan	Information Plan
Electrical Plan	Systems Plan
Plumbing Plan	Technology Plan

Figure 4.2 An analogy for understanding IT architecture.

This definition, for example, might serve our purposes:

> IT ar•chi•tec•ture n. 1. The art and science of planning and design-ing target information technology infrastructures for a business. 2. Technological structures as a whole. 3. A style and method of designing and planning these technological structures <Kerr Systems International's *IT Architecture Methodology*>. 4. The exist-ing information systems environment <the company's *de facto* IT *architecture*>.

With these two generic definitions, we have the makings of a solid architec-ture analogy (see Figure 4.2). The former tells us that building architecture is "the art and science of designing and erecting buildings," while the latter suggests that IT architecture is "the art and science of planning and designing a target comput-ing infrastructure for a business." Now, let us examine the details.

THE ESSENCE OF ARCHITECTURES

Architectures are plans. Specifically, they are plans for building what an "owner" wants. In the case of building architecture, the owner (be it an individual or a huge multinational conglomerate) determines the type of structure to be built. The cor-responding architecture is a set of plans that define such details as site layout, floor plan design, and heating, electricity, and plumbing systems.

In the case of a RITA, the owner is a firm's management team. The resultant IT architecture comprises a set of initiatives for delivering the information, appli-cations, and computing hardware needed to support management's vision for the future.

These initiatives, articulated as projects and programs, frame the RITA for the enterprise. In turn, all these projects and programs will be put into priority order for execution within the firm's program-centric strategic planning process (as described in Chapter 2).

BEST PRACTICES BUSINESS IN ACTION

Creating a Fast-Food IT Architecture at Dunkin' Brands, Inc.

Dunkin' Brands, Inc., a division of Allied Domecq, has three fast-food chains under its corporate umbrella: Dunkin' Donuts, Baskin-Robbins, and Togo's (a popular West Coast sandwich shop chain).

A key growth strategy for the firm calls for selling all three brands under one roof. Today, Dunkin' Brands, Inc. has over 12,000 outlets, with 1,100 being multi-brand stores. More are planned. The challenge is providing the infrastructure needed to support continued growth.

Information technology certainly has a role to play. The company is investing more than $10 million in its information systems architecture (ISA) plan, which calls for the creation of a distributed point-of-sale (POS) system and the development of a backbone network and support applications needed to make it hum.

As the ISA plan is implemented, the firm and its franchisees will be provided with:

- Online access to sales, inventory, and profitability data
- An automated inventory replenishment process
- Important management reporting on such minutiae as sales per brand, sales per square foot, and regional demand trends

Dunkin' Brands, with the adoption of a RITA-like approach to supporting a multi-brand corporate strategy, is another example of a successful business adjusting its practices in order to continue to be successful in a *Best Practices World*.

Source: Based on information provided on the website: www.allieddomecq.com/en/AboutUs/ OurBusiness/CorporateStrategy/Portfolio.htm, September 28, 2004.

A quick review of the Dunkin' Brands sidebar shows how one early best practices adapter is proceeding with RITA development.

With Resilience Built In

It is a fact that every organization that uses automation has an IT architecture in place. Most of these architectures *were not* created deliberately but are *de facto*. They have evolved over time from stand-alone implementations. For this reason, many firms are suffering from the results of an unstable IT environment that is difficult to change and slow to respond to emerging business needs—unable to withstand the demands of the global marketplace of the early 21st century.

With a *Best Practices Enterprise*™ approach, IT architecture must be designed deliberately with resilience built in—capable of rapid change and extensibility. Lesser IT architectures have not fully contemplated the flexibility needs of the organization that they serve. These kinds of architecture lead to instability and chaos when adjusted or changed.

RITA design is a process by which businesses can plan, forge, and field data, systems, and computing technology assets in a readily modifiable and sustainable way. Take a look at the Bowne & Co. sidebar for a glimpse of what firms are already doing to hedge their bets.

So, How Do You Build a Resilient IT Architecture?

Now that you are convinced that a well-thought-out RITA is an important thing for an organization to have, one question still remains, "How do you build one?" It is straightforward enough: answer three simple questions about the IT environment:

- What is the state of your IT environment today?
- Where do you want it to be tomorrow?
- What work is needed to establish the IT environment envisioned?

BEST PRACTICES BUSINESS IN ACTION
Boning Up on Computing Resilience at Bowne & Co.

Bowne & Co., Inc. provides financial printing, digital printing, and electronic delivery services to some of the world's largest publicly traded companies, banks, and investment firms. The company produces such items as mutual fund statements and annual reports as well as merger and acquisition and initial public offering documentation.

Interestingly, Bowne & Co. is one of the first enterprises to pursue the use of IBM's grid and autonomic computing services, which help companies to both exploit their disparate computing power (by reconstituting it to work as a virtual, single, large computer) and implement the computing environment to be self-configuring and self-protecting.

The *Statements* software application was the first one piloted by Bowne. A core system, it delivers critical financial statements to customers. The firm achieved a 50% productivity improvement through the effort—demonstrating that these emerging technologies can significantly improve IT infrastructure utilization while enhancing the ability to quickly respond to client needs.

With these kinds of capabilities budding in the marketplace, and firms like Bowne & Co. proving their viability, *Best Practices Era* organizations will be better positioned to establish computing environments that are readily enhanced and ever resilient.

Source: Based on *IBM Expands Grid and Autonomic Computing Services: Bowne & Co. Grid Project Improves Performance of Key Company Applications*, IBM Press Release, December 12, 2003.

Many IT professionals have yet to recognize that RITA work boils down to answering these three questions. With the aid of a solid RITA methodology, such as the one described in the next section, any enterprise can build one.

THE RITA METHODOLOGY

RITAs comprise four basic dimensions, which include:

- *Work*—the work performed by the organization
- *Information*—the data needed to perform the work
- *Applications*—the automated systems needed to manage the data
- *Technology*—the computing and communication devices needed to run the systems

Knowing where a firm is today (a baseline architecture) and where it wants to be (a target architecture) across these four dimensions is a key part of developing an initial RITA (see Figure 4.3).

With that said, let us explore each of the dimensions and learn how they interact.

Work Dimension

When working within this dimension, two questions that must be answered include "How is work performed today?" and "How should work be performed in the future?" The first is answered by defining the current organization design, personnel job titles, descriptions, and process workflow. The second is answered by determining the logical business operations, worker types, and work locations. Essentially, we document the dynamics of the current work environment and decide upon the "who, what, and where" of the target workplace.

A full understanding of the work dimension is crucial to the success of the entire IT architecture design effort because it provides the necessary link between the other three architectural dimensions. Without a clear picture of the current work environment and the underpinnings of its future vision, we have no context for the subsequent information, application, and technology strategies developed through the RITA process.

It is through these interdependencies that the RITA methodology delivers an IT plan that maps directly to the strategic plan of the organization. After all, it is the integration of the strategic plan and IT plan that will provide an organization with the foundation that it needs to fully exploit information technology to competitive gain.

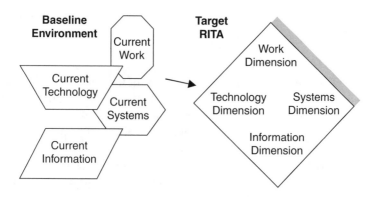

Figure 4.3 Work begins with a baseline assessment of the individual elements of the IT environment before an integrated RITA can be defined.

Information Dimension

Answering the questions of "What information is currently used by the business?" and "What information will be needed in the future?" is the driver behind this dimension. These questions can be answered by first documenting current data file structures (both automated and manual), data volumes, and information characteristics and then defining the target information subjects, data entities, and integrated database environment needed to support the target information management view of the business.

It is here that we begin to understand the breadth of change that may be needed within an organization's information management environment to support the future direction of the business. For example, natural systems that manually manage data may need to be converted into a computerized format in order for the firm to realize its strategic vision, and some of the existing automated databases may need to be updated in order to make the information they store easily accessible by personnel throughout the organization.

Applications Dimension

The applications view of RITA work asks the organization to specify "What automated systems are in use today?" and "What applications are needed to support the target business environment of tomorrow?" Current application portfolios, user satisfaction surveys, and computer program characteristics are used to describe today's systems, while automation opportunities lists, systems integration strategies, and target application portfolios define future needs.

By understanding the gaps between the installed base of applications and the systems needed by the enterprise, a firm can develop a systems plan that will move the concern from where it is today to where it must be tomorrow in order to achieve its goals.

Technology Dimension

The technology dimension is typically the easiest of the four views for businesses to "get their arms around." This is due, in part, to the computer industry's emphasis on "boxes and pipes." Most computer vendors freely offer advice regarding system upgrades and migration plans, making a majority of IT professionals well versed in computing hardware options.

Current hardware inventories, usage statistics, and processing capacities are the mainspring of the baseline technology environment, while target site hardware configurations, the placement of applications, and target standards suites accent the technology futures dimension of RITA design work.

As Figure 4.4 denotes, it is the integration of the work, information, applications, and technology dimensions that comprise a RITA. Any one of the views alone does not a RITA make. Many companies offering services in this arena confuse clients by offering to build only part of the picture and calling that an IT architecture. Do not fall into that trap. A RITA has four dimensions—and a firm needs all four to support its business.

With this as a foundation, let us look at the methodology work steps that go into actually producing an industrial-strength RITA.

A SIX-STEP APPROACH

There are six phases or work steps in a RITA methodology. They include:

- RITA framework
- Baseline characterization
- Target definition
- Opportunities identification
- Implementation planning
- RITA administration

Each phase produces a distinct set of deliverables. When completed, the composite of these deliverables constitutes the RITA. Here is how it works.

RITA Framework

A RITA development project begins with the *RITA framework* phase. This phase starts by addressing basic project *housekeeping*—namely, ensuring that there is a full-time RITA team in place and an ESC ready to oversee the initiative. With the right project execution elements in place, RITA work may begin.

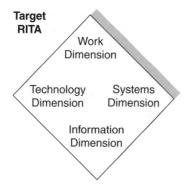

Figure 4.4 The four dimensions of a RITA plan.

The RITA framework phase produces an architectural framework document. It contains an overview of the organization's business goals and strategic drivers and presents a set of architectural principles. These principles are statements of executive preferences regarding the way information systems and technology will be planned, developed, and deployed throughout an organization. They become the "rules of the road" for the RITA effort.

An example of an architectural principle may be as simple as:

Data will be stored once and as close to the end-user as possible.

to something more dramatic such as:

Every customer service center business activity will be fully automated.

Regardless of their content, architectural principles help to steady a firm's grip on what it wants its future IT environment to be and how it wants it to work.

Once the principles are defined, it is important for an organization to document the rationale for, and the implications of, adopting each one. Crafting the rationale is a straightforward activity. By doing so, the organization is addressing the question "Why is this principle important to our business?"

For example, the rationale for the "data stored once" principle might be:

Entering and storing data once establishes a single authoritative source of information. This authoritative source will provide the consistency and quality needed for confident decision making within the organization.

Worker productivity will be improved by providing accurate information needed to do one's job. Time spent collecting and reconciling data will be minimized as data become more accurate and readily accessible.

While the rationale discussion tends to be simple enough to develop because its intention is to state the importance of the principle to the organization, documenting the implications of adopting each principle requires a little more thought because the implications often translate into new projects and programs to be included in the RITA implementation plan. If the implications are not appropriately identified, then there is a great possibility that the value of the principle will never be realized by the concern.

Continuing with our example, consider the implications of the "data is stored once" principle. The implications may include the need to establish a:

- Common data-naming convention (to reduce the likelihood of unintended redundancy)
- Hardware infrastructure in which to store the data appropriately
- Data administrator function to track and manage the data
- Sophisticated database management system to store and access the data
- Training program to assist the business community in using the data appropriately

If a firm lacks any of these elements, new project initiatives would have to be established and made part of the RITA implementation plan. While some may be inclined to dismiss principles definition work as "just more motherhood and apple pie," it is important to resist the temptation. A well-defined RITA framework provides an organization with the depth and detail it needs to manage the evolution of its technology environment.

Baseline Characterization

A *baseline characterization document* is produced next. It contains a summary of the firm's current operational, information management, applications, and technology environments. These, as discussed earlier in this chapter, are the four views of RITA.

The data that characterize these four dimensions of the current environment are captured in a series of templates that cross-reference the four views to one another. For example, the systems in place today are cross-referenced to the data files that they manipulate, the data files are cross-referenced to the business functions that require the data, the business functions are cross-referenced to information technology that are installed at the business locations; and so on (see a sample presented in Figure 4.5).

Application \ Data	Client	Product	Sales	Store	Supplier	Vendor	Trucking	Account	Insurance	Regulations	Financial
Sales Tracking	X				X	X					X
Customer Support		X						X	X		
Inventory System			X	X	X			X			
G/L System			X								
R&D Tracking										X	
MIS			X							X	X

Figure 4.5 Sample baseline template excerpt.

The typical RITA methodology employs over 15 different templates in constructing a *baseline characterization*; together they are intended to paint a clear picture of how an enterprise currently exploits IT resources.

The document concludes with a *baseline assessment section* that describes those areas of the current environment that are well done and should be considered for inclusion in the target architecture as well as those areas of the baseline environment that are in need of improvement.

What is striking about baseline assessment work is that it usually points to issues that personnel within the organization already know and understand. It almost goes without stating the obvious; however, what were once only hunches about the current work environment are now supported by data gleaned through the baseline analysis.

It should be noted that, in general, the opinions presented in a baseline assessment reflect what staff members *believe is actually* happening within a firm's work environment.

While it is important to have examples to illustrate important points about the current work setting, such should not be construed as a "search for the guilty" or a "finger-pointing" exercise—to allow that to happen would be to miss the point, which is simply to document where the concern is today in regard to technology use.

Target Definition

With the baseline characterization as the firm's strategic plan as a backdrop, the *target definition* phase is best started by preparing a blank sheet of paper and asking the RITA project team to paint their vision for the future deployment of information technology within the company.

The RITA team should not be encumbered by past practice and traditions. In essence, the future can be anything that the team thinks it should be to help the organization reach its goals. The team is encouraged to "think out of the box." It is outside the artificial boundaries created within organizations that truly creative business solutions are contrived—sometimes even defining the identity of a business (see the Wells Fargo sidebar for an example).

It is not unusual to develop over 20 target templates that, like the baseline templates, cross-reference the four architectural dimensions. The *business systems to hardware template*, for example, cross-references target business systems to target hardware platforms. This shows how the systems will be spread across the target hardware environment. Another template cross-references the target work functions against the logical work locations. This defines what kind of work is performed at which business sites.

BEST PRACTICES BUSINESS IN ACTION
The CEO Portal at Wells Fargo

A far cry from the stagecoach days of yesteryear, Wells Fargo & Co. is reinventing itself, yet again. The bank is developing an entirely new suite of computing capabilities that will redefine its business.

The Commercial Electronic Office Business Portal (CEO Portal) is one of Wells Fargo's many recent innovations. It offers middle-market and corporate customers cash management, credit, international, trust, and investment services through a single website.

Additionally, subscribers not only can adjust the "look and feel" of the portal on the computer desktop, but they can also add and modify the products and services that they want to acquire from the bank with the click of the mouse. In the past, such customized adjustments required phone calls to the bank.

Wells Fargo hopes that such ease-of-use will work to differentiate the bank from the fierce competition that has besieged the banking industry since deregulation. With features such as event messaging, which allow the customer to set parameters and decide which transactions (e.g., wire processing, unauthorized transmittal, or stop payment notices) they want to be notified about and self-administration capabilities that allow such activities as fraud filtering and credit management, the CEO portal is sure to attract attention.

By rethinking its use of computing technology, Wells Fargo is establishing itself as a premier *Best Practices Enterprise™*. It is allowing its customers to do business with the bank on their terms and is developing the automation capabilities needed to propel the organization well into the 21st century.

Source: Based on "Real Simple," by Ivan Schneider, *Bank Systems & Technology*, www.banktech.com, January 30, 2005.

It is of extreme importance that the team considers issues about systems resilience needs and alternate deployment scenarios during this phase of RITA development work. It is here that such foundational elements are "designed-in" to the architecture plan. Remember, a firm will need a highly flexible and extensible technology environment in order to compete in the *Best Practices Era*.

A successful *Best Practices Enterprise*™ must have a vision for its computing environment that includes the capabilities to "change on a dime." Take a look at Appendix B to see an example of a target definition document from industry. It shows how a firm goes about developing such capabilities.

Opportunities Identification

With the current environment defined through the baseline templates and the target architecture conveyed through the target ones, the next step is to determine the projects that are necessary to move the organization from its existing environment to its vision for the future.

A "gap analysis" is performed in the *opportunities identification* phase. The analysis is the starting point for the project identification. It requires that the RITA Team compare the baseline with the target and identify what is missing (i.e., "gaps") between them. Each gap translates into a potential project or program. Major differences between the baseline and target perspectives translate into the strategic initiatives that comprise the RITA implementation plan.

For instance, an organization that currently uses dated data management tools and wants to establish an integrated database environment that will support the latest in e-commerce capabilities in the future may need to embark on an initiative that includes several projects such as:

- Data management package selection and implementation
- Establishment of the DBA function
- Hiring and training of e-commerce development staff
- Identifying and conducting the appropriate pilot project(s)

All of the potential projects identified in this phase are documented in a standard format that includes important elements such as project name, description, dependencies, strategic significance, and other related issues. This information is an important input to the *implementation planning* phase that follows it.

Implementation Planning

This phase of the RITA methodology is performed in two parts. The first part takes the project opportunities identified in the previous phase and organizes them into three tiers or *implementation plateaus*. The second part produces first-cut project plans for those projects that fall into the first plateau.

The most important projects (based on strategic significance and project interdependences) are placed in Plateau I and the next most important fall into Plateau II, with the remainder becoming Plateau III projects.

The plateaus span the organization's planning horizon time frame. For example, the Federal Government uses a 7-year planning horizon, and most commercial organizations use a 5-year time frame. Using the 5-year planning horizon as the model, Plateau I projects are those scheduled to commence in the first 18 months, Plateau II projects are those that begin in months 19 through 36, and Plateau III projects are those beginning in months 37 and beyond.

Because of the dynamic nature of organizations, first-cut project plans are not developed for Plateau II and III projects. After all, too much may change in 18 months to warrant the development of plans for projects that may never see the "light of day." However, first-cut plans should be developed for Plateau I projects and programs.

The same project planning template presented in Chapter 2 (for use in program-centric strategic planning) can be used here to plan the IT-related efforts. As you may recall from Chapter 2, that template should include such information as:

- Project/program name
- Objectives
- Enablers
- Task lists
- Special skills required
- Effectiveness measures

- Description
- Critical success factors
- Constraints
- Delivery schedule
- Special tools required
- Completion criteria

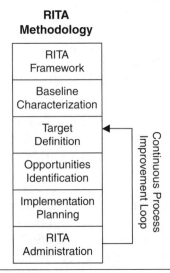

Figure 4.6 The RITA methodology's continuous process improvement loop.

These first-cut plans are a handy way for the RITA development team to pass on their insights to the project managers that will follow (more on this in subsequent chapters). They provide a "headstart" in developing the detailed project plans that will be needed to execute the stated initiatives.

As a final note, the collection of these project plans and the implementation time-line constitute the RITA implementation plan that will be used to establish the IT environment needed to support the business. In a *Best Practices World*, where program-centric strategic planning is in place, the resultant RITA implementation plan becomes just another program to be managed within an organization's strategic plan.

BEST PRACTICES BUSINESS IN ACTION
Driving Sponsor Reviews at the Headquarters of the Marine Corps

Recently, I led a project team at the United States Marine Corps (USMC). The team consisted exclusively of Marine Corps colonels and majors (which is equivalent to middle management in a corporate setting). Our charge was straightforward: develop a RITA implementation plan that will lead the Corps well into the 21st century. No small feat, given that the Marine Corps spans the globe and is several hundred thousand strong.

As you can imagine, a project of this size and scope cannot be taken lightly. Sponsor review meetings (SRMs) became particularly important during this engagement. Our SRMs were attended by two- and three-star generals from across the USMC headquarters in Washington, D.C. All functional areas of the Corps were represented within this group.

The fact that the USMC's highest-ranking people participated in these meetings (held every 3 weeks) was a strong testament to the Marines' dedication to the project. The top brass knew that this effort was about redefining the systems environment for the USMC, and they wanted to be sure to impact the result.

For example, our team was having difficulties engaging the Aviation Division of the Corps in the RITA development effort. One quick reference to that fact during our 10:00 a.m. briefing changed the project immensely. By 11:45 a.m. that morning, the RITA team had received three separate telephone calls from various marine aviators all wanting to participate in our project. Now, that is management commitment!

When all was said and done, the Marine Corps had built a comprehensive RITA. The plan contains 63 new projects and programs, which span all types of technology- and operations-related topics from ground-to-satellite communications and tactical defense systems to Marine Corps business process redesign (BPR) initiatives.

The $318 million implementation effort is well under way.

RITA Administration

RITA administration development is the last phase of the RITA methodology. When done properly, it yields a process for ensuring that the IT architecture remains synchronized with the strategic direction of the organization—an important *continuous process improvement* step that is often overlooked otherwise (see Figure 4.6).

BEST PRACTICES BUSINESS IN ACTION

Coors Brewing Company's On-Demand IT Infrastructure

Over the past 10 years, Coors Brewing Company has doubled in size. The third largest domestic brewer, Coors sells over a dozen varieties of beer in 30 markets around the globe. Its focus on growth and profitability has led the company to re-think its position on managing and maintaining the non-core elements of its business—those activities that are not directly related to the manufacturing and distribution of its beer.

With the help of Electronic Data Systems (EDS), it was decided that the IT functions would be a good place to begin the analysis. As a precursor to the outsourcing arrangement, time was spent developing a detailed IT architecture plan. In this way, any implications related to the decision to contract out computing support functions could be understood and discussed more intelligently.

It was through IT architecture work that Coors decided to enter into a new pact with EDS. The brewer designated EDS to manage its back office information technology operations, including systems maintenance, help desk services, and IT operations. The move created new opportunities for Coors to reduce its cost of operations, improve systems dependability, and enhance business unit applications support.

More importantly, with the anticipation of rapid globalization of the business as a backdrop, the EDS arrangement positions Coors to be able to regulate its IT infrastructure like never before—gaining an unprecedented opportunity to scale computing capacity to match business volumes, without incurring the costs of carrying large amounts of overhead in order to do it.

Early results have shown promise, with a:

- 70% reduction in application maintenance costs
- 40% reduction in new systems development costs
- $1.2 million savings in IT resources

As the firm anxiously eyes its future, these kinds of advances will be critical for continued success in enhancing Coors' presence in the markets that it serves. For us, it is encouraging to see how firms are employing best practices, such as resilient IT architecture design, to advance their causes.

Source: Based on information provided on the website:
www.eds.com/services/casestudies/coors.aspx, October 12, 2005.

Typically, a three-pronged approach is taken to ensure that the RITA always reflects the direction that the organization is heading toward the actualization of its business goals and objectives. The approach includes:

- *RITA administration function definition*—The assignment of personnel to keep the RITA synchronized with the organization's business vision
- *RITA administration procedure determination*—The establishment of a set of operating procedures necessary for updating the RITA implementation plan
- *Communication vehicle identification*—The appointment of support mechanisms needed to ensure that the status of each of the RITA projects and programs is communicated throughout the organization and that senior management is involved in determining the IT priorities of the firm

With this said, it is not unusual for an enterprise to establish a project management office (PMO) within its IT function to oversee the execution of the RITA implementation plan. Regularly scheduled project coordination meetings are typically held by the PMO as a means of monitoring and coaching project managers and their teams in project management and implementation.

A myriad of communication vehicles, such as newsletters, intranet sites, sponsor review meetings, and post-project assessment documents, tend to emerge, as well, as means of improving cross-project and cross-company knowledge sharing and transfer. Communication is an essential element of RITA administration. In fact, it can make or break a RITA implementation (see the Marine Corps sidebar for an example).

It is important to note that these components are described and presented in the *RITA administration document* deliverable, and the implementation of the various elements of the RITA administration process (i.e., function, procedures, and communication vehicles) often becomes additional projects included in the RITA implementation plan's first implementation plateau.

Once a RITA is in place, an organization has a valuable management tool in its possession. It can and should be used to inform an organization's IT decision-making. It can even be used to assist in such matters as outsourcing and off-shoring, both popular IT alternatives in today's business environment (see the Coors Brewing sidebar for more).

IN CLOSING

Clearly, robust and easily modifiable automation is fundamental to achieving a firm's vision for the future in the *Best Practices Enterprise*™ business environment. A resilient information systems architecture is needed to ensure that the automation fits the business that it intends to support. Once the work, the information, the applications, and the technology (needed to fulfill the strategic business goals and objectives of the enterprise) are organized to fit seamlessly together, the RITA becomes a blueprint for success. And a blueprint it is!

Building a RITA is a lot like constructing a building. Both disciplines provide plans for assembling things. Both should be driven by their respective "owners." Both must integrate different components into a unified whole to be truly effective.

RITA development work requires the careful execution of a thorough RITA methodology that harnesses executive involvement, defines the current business and IT environments, and identifies the implementation plans needed to realize the target IT architecture. Once completed, the RITA must be kept current with shifts in business priorities and direction through an "executive-sanctioned" administration process.

Finally, businesses that embark on RITA work can gain a competitive edge due, in part, to the improvements in systems resilience and flexibility, quality, IT expense reduction, and better time-to-market with new products and services. However, such benefits do not come without their price. Hard work and management commitment are needed to build the kind of integrated IT architecture plans that will make a difference.

In the next chapter, we will explore the project management components that are essential execution elements of both program-centric strategic planning and resilient IT architecture.

* * *

Appendix B

SAMPLE RESILIENT IT ARCHITECTURE TARGET DEFINITION DOCUMENT (XYZ INSURANCE CORPORATION)

In this, the third phase of the "Resilient IT Architecture Project," a target definition document, has been produced. It presents the XYZ Insurance Corporation's
(XYZ) target IT architecture. This architecture was created by:

- Reviewing the baseline assessment of the *de facto* IT architecture
- Determining potential responses to the shortcomings of the *de facto*
  IT architecture
- Developing architectural models that represent those responses
- Completing a series of templates that further detail the architectural
  models and show the integration and interdependences among them

The target architecture is presented across four dimensions, including an
operations view, an information view, an applications view, and an information
technology view (see Figure B.1).

These four views (or models) are tied together in this document to ensure that
the department has a solid foundation on which to build as it evolves toward its
vision for the future.

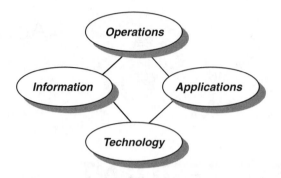

Figure B.1 The four views of IT architecture.

MORE ABOUT ARCHITECTURE

The four views of RITA can be thought of as being analogous to the detailed architectural blueprints and specifications for the subassemblies of a building. For example,

- A site plan is like an operations view.
- A floor plan is like an information view.
- An electrical plan is like an application view.
- A plumbing plan is like a technology view.

The bottom line on architectures for buildings (and for IT) is providing a minimum but rigorous set of architectural renderings which will allow the building (or IT environment) to be developed in a way which will allow the most flexibility for the tenants (or system users), while constraining the detailed designs required to ensure that the desired style and characteristics of the building (or the IT environment) are maintained over time.

The following is a RITA team's architectural rendering for the IT environment at XYZ.

TARGET VIEWS

As described in Figure B.1, there are four views or dimensions of RITA:

- Target operations
- Target information
- Target applications
- Target information technology

The content of each of these views is presented in the following sections.

Operations View

The operations view of a RITA provides a normalized view of the work of the department. The first step in developing the operations view of a RITA is to break down each business function into its logical components of work or conceptual operations groups (COGs). COGs will be used throughout the rest of this document.

It should be noted that a COG is not associated with the current organizational structure, "reporting lines," the person performing the work, or any physical location. It essence, it is a generic bundle of work that is independent of the organization in which it is performed.

This distinction allows a COG to be defined by the output (or service) for which it is conceptually responsible and the activities it must perform to achieve that output without regard to who or what might do that work within the organization today. In essence, COGs become fundamental building blocks for defining a normalized work model of the business.

Once the building blocks are defined, they can be grouped together into a value chain that represents all the work that is done by a department to achieve its corporate mission.

The XYZ Insurance Corporation value chain

The XYZ value chain (presented in Figure B.2) can be thought of as containing the network of COGs that constitute the department. As Figure B.2 suggests, the value chain begins with the business mission and ends with customers. The value chain that resides between the two is the work that is done to deliver the "value" expected.

The XYZ value chain is divided into five distinct components:

- *Plan*—contains a collection of generic processes that support the XYZ planning activities
- *Staff*—contains a collection of generic processes that support XYZ staffing activities
- *Train*—contains a collection of generic processes that support XYZ training activities
- *Perform*—contains a collection of processes that support XYZ key performance activities
- *Support*—contains a collection of generic processes that are performed in the provision of activities supporting XYZ

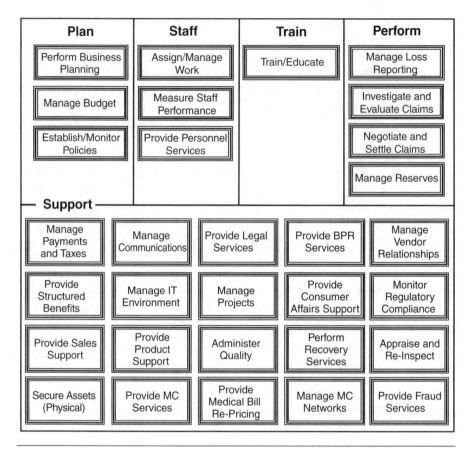

Figure B.2 The XYZ value chain.

This value chain represents all of the work activities performed by XYZ. Below is a discussion of each of the business processes that make up the XYZ value chain.

Planning element.
The plan component contains the processes that support XYZ planning activities. The generic processes include:

- Perform business planning
- Manage budget
- Establish/monitor policies/practices

Staffing element.
The staff component contains the processes that support XYZ staffing activities. The generic processes include:

- Assign/manage work
- Perform performance measurement
- Provide personnel services

Training element.
The train component contains the processes that support XYZ training activities. The generic process includes:

- Train/educate

Performance element.
The perform component contains the processes that support XYZ performance activities. The generic processes include:

- Manage loss reporting
- Investigate and evaluate claim
- Negotiate/settle claim
- Establish/maintain reserve
- Measure/monitor loss cost

Support element.
The support component contains a collection of processes performed in support of XYZ. The generic processes include:

- Manage communications
- Manage projects
- Manage managed care networks
- Manage payments/refunds
- Administer quality measurements
- Provide process improvement services
- Provide product development support
- Provide recovery services
- Manage vendors and relationships
- Provide legal services
- Provide sales/customer support
- Secure physical assets
- Maintain IT environment
- Monitor regulatory compliance
- Provide consumer affairs support
- Provide managed care services
- Provide fraud ID services
- Provide appraisal and re-inspection services
- Manage structured benefits
- Provide medical bill re-pricing services

Note: A detailed discussion of each of the COGs listed above is included in sections relating to the deliverables of this document.

To complete the operations view

While the value chain and its COGs provide the foundation of the operations view of XYZ's information system architecture, the operations view is further detailed through a set of associated templates that cross-reference the COGs to various elements of the other architectural views (i.e., information, applications, and technology).

The templates needed to complete the understanding of the operations view include:

- Target COGs to user class affinity matrix
- Target COGs to current organization matrix
- Target COGs to target applications
- Target COGs to data grouping

These are discussed in detail in a later section of this document. Copies of the completed templates may also be found in the deliverables sections.

Information View

The information view of a RITA logically groups data into subject areas that are representative of the information needed to support the core business functions of the department.

There are 11 subject areas identified in XYZ's information view. Each subject area contains an illustrative set of data groups to demonstrate the type of information that can be found in that subject area. XYZ's subject areas include:

1. *Claim*
   - Loss event/accident
   - Claim file strategy
   - Claim information
   - Appraisal/inspection
   - Claimant
   - Damage
   - Recovered property
   - Injury
   - Quality rating
   - Loss party

2. *Product*
   - Contract
   - Coverage
   - Trade/industry

3. *Customer*
   - Insured
   - Claim history
   - Account information
   - Agency
   - Special instructions
   - Policy information
   - Demographics

4. *Medical*
   - PPOs
   - Diagnosis
   - Rehabilitation/treatment
   - Fee schedule
   - Prognosis

5. *Legal*
   - Statutes
   - Legal case strategy
   - State agency
   - Legal procedures
   - Courts
   - Legal motion
   - Deposition
   - Regulatory
   - Trade/industry

6. *Investigation*
   - Witness
   - Responsible party
   - Intelligence gathered

7. *Financial*
   - Expenses and budgets
   - Payments
   - Liabilities/bills
   - Reserves
   - Salvage/subrogation/refund transactions
   - Annuity information

8. *Employee*
   - Employee information
   - Workload
   - Training and education

9. Business area
- Workgroup
- Business policies and procedures
- Productivity
- Business rules information

10. Provider
- Service
- Service provider

11. IT assets
- Computer security
- Hardware/software inventory

Seamless access to data is imperative

Although the content of each subject area has not been exhaustively defined (certainly, further analysis will be needed for a comprehensive enterprise data model to be created), the list does serve as an illustration of the type of information required by the department.

Yet, as Figure B.3 suggests, the most important point of the information view is to highlight the need for the department's target data management environment to be built in such a way as to provide easy access to the core applications that support the business activities performed by XYZ.

To complete the information view

While the subject areas and their data groups provide the foundation of the information view of XYZ's RITA, the information view is further detailed through a set of associated templates that cross-reference the data groups to various elements of the other architectural views (i.e., operations, applications, and technology). The templates needed to complete understanding of the information view include:

- Target application to data grouping affinity matrix
- Characteristics of information
- Data groups to level of computing
- Target COGs to data grouping

These templates are discussed in detail in a later section of this document. Copies of the completed templates can be found in the deliverables sections.

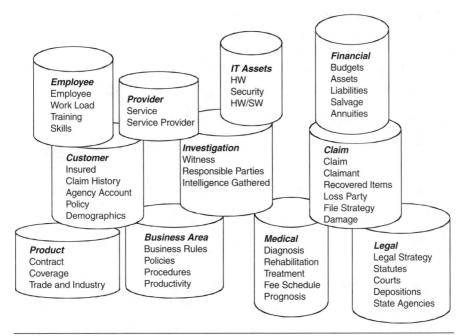

Figure B.3 The information view.

Applications View

The applications view of a RITA identifies the business systems that must be put into place to support the work performed and manage the data used by the department. There are 14 target applications identified in XYZ's application view:

1. *Business planning system with*
   - Budget management subsystem
   - Project management subsystem

2. *Claim handling system with*
   - Loss reporting and assignment subsystem
   - Investigation and determination subsystem
   - Appraisal/re-inspection component
   - Fraud identification expert system component
   - Negotiation and settlement subsystem
   - Structured benefits component
   - Payment/refund management component
   - Reserve management subsystem

3. *Medical claim support system (tied to claim handling system) with*
   - Managed care support subsystem
   - Medical bill re-pricing subsystem
   - Managed care network subsystem

4. *Recovery management system (tied to claim handling system)*

5. *Legal case management system (tied to claim handling system)*

6. *Departmental policy/procedures database (accessible from all business applications)*

7. *Rules/regulations database (accessible from all business applications)*

8. *Customer database (accessible from all applications)*

9. *Work-in-process (WIP) subsystem (sits on top of all core business applications)*

10. *Quality/performance measurement subsystem (sits on top of all core business applications)*

11. *Vendor tracking system*

12. *Human resources system with*
    - Training component
    - Hire/terminate component
    - Staff tracking component
    - Career development component

13. *Consumer affairs tracking system*

14. *Physical asset inventory system*

The interconnections among these target applications are presented in *Figure B.4.*

A SINGLE SYSTEM VIEW IS THE GOAL

As Figure B.4 suggests, XYZ's target applications are tied together logically to provide the business user with the appearance of a single system that supports all of the automation needs of the department.

A set of integrated claim handling applications acts as the hub of the applications view. It is here that all related work is triggered. An intelligence layer surrounds this hub and each of the related applications. A work-in-process (WIP)

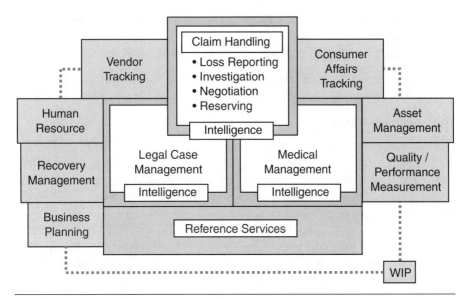

Figure B.4 The applications view.

application is woven through all of the systems providing XYZ with an ability to manage and monitor the department's workflow.

A set of "reference services" that contain rules and regulations, customer, and policy and procedure information rounds out the target application environment.

TO COMPLETE THE APPLICATIONS VIEW

Although this graphical representation provides the foundation of the applications view of XYZ's RITA, the applications view is further detailed through a set of associated templates that cross-reference the applications to various elements of the other architectural views (i.e., operations, information, and technology). The templates needed to complete understanding of the applications view include:

- Target application to data grouping affinity matrix
- Application characteristics
- Target application to level of computing
- Target COGs to target applications
- Target application to target application (integration opportunities)
- Target application to existing application (integration opportunities)
- Target applications to user class
- Target applications access by physical location

- Application to generic application environments (GAE) affinity matrix
- Target application to client/server implementation type

These templates are discussed in detail in a later section of this document. Copies of the completed templates can also be found in the deliverables sections.

Technology View

The technology view of a RITA identifies the "boxes and pipes" needed to run the automated systems. The technology view describes the styles of computing to be used to implement the systems and shows how the systems and the data will be dispersed across the communications and computing infrastructure within the department.

As described in the department's strategic framework document, published last year, XYZ's target technology view will be standardized to support the department's need for interoperability of the systems and the supporting computing and communications hardware platforms.

A three-level network computing infrastructure is envisioned

Figure B.5 shows the technology topology to be a three-tiered network computing environment. Such an environment has multiple computer platforms interconnected by communications network hardware and software. There are three basic "levels" of computing, with a variation on the third, allowing for remote and/or mobile computing: enterprise, workgroup, individual, and mobile (a special case of individual).

Enterprise.

Enterprise-level systems are those applications which are used by practically all XYZ employees. The enterprise-level systems will reside at a single location (probably the current data center). All users will have access to this enterprise level and the application systems it supports via a network connection to their individual workstation (see Figure B.6 to better understand how the applications will be dispersed across the enterprise and work group levels of computing).

Workgroup.

Workgroup systems provide functionality and data access which are only used by a subset of the department's workforce and processes. This subset, referred to as a workgroup, is composed of individuals who share common requirements and needs for information access to perform their business processes. There are multiple workgroups within XYZ. They typically have a need for quick access to current, process-specific information.

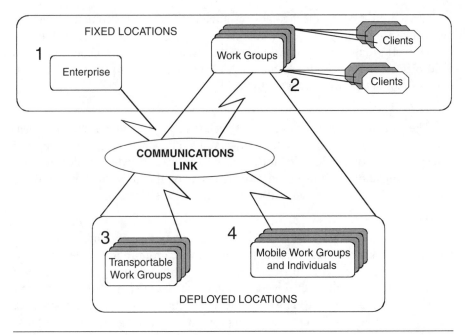

Figure B.5   The target technology view.

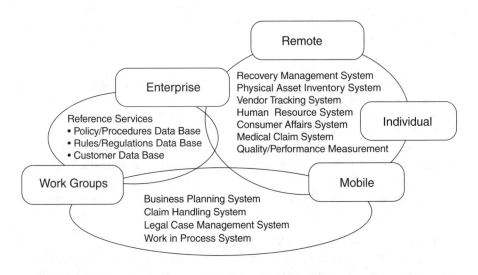

Figure B.6   The dispersion of target applications across computing levels.

If required, the target technology resource will provide for computer processing in close proximity to the workgroup to support these quick-access requirements. Workgroup-level systems will be deployed to physical locations (such as field offices or specific floors within XYZ headquarters) to support a critical mass of individuals within a workgroup.

Individual.

The individual level of the target technology view equips an individual worker with a workstation which is networked to allow access to workgroup and enterprise technology facilities for access to applications which reside at those levels. Application systems which actually reside on the individual level will fall largely into the groupware and office automation classifications.

Mobile.

Mobile is a *special case* of the individual level of computing, in which an individual worker requires access to individual, workgroup, and/or enterprise systems while away from XYZ offices. The typical hardware configuration will be a laptop version of the individual workstation, outfitted with a modem and communications software, which allows remote connectivity to department systems, although other access devices may be appropriate, depending on the characteristics of the envisioned user community and the services which will be accessed by this community.

Three tiers of network connectivity will be in place

To support these three levels of computing, there will be three tiers of network connectivity: local area networks (LANs), campus area networks (CANs), and wide area networks (WANs). These three tiers of network connectivity are described below.

Local area networks (LANS).

LANs are used for kiosk and/or workstation access to individual, workgroup, or enterprise computing resources and for providing file and peripheral sharing. A LAN also provides communication with members of the local workgroup via electronic mail (e-mail), local office automation tools, and simple localized application systems which run either on the workstations themselves or on LAN-based processors (referred to as LAN servers). The LAN will always provide the link to other network components, which in turn will link to other computer processors. The only probable exception would be in the case of mobile computing at the individual level, in which direct LAN connectivity may not be feasible.

Campus area networks (CANs).

CANs are used for interconnecting LANs within a large physical work location, such as the corporate office or across a "campus" of multiple buildings which are in close proximity to each other, such as a headquarters complex. Each major fixed physical location will have a single CAN as a "backbone." CANs will support higher speeds than LANs for rapid message and file transfer between loosely coupled applications which run on multiple workgroup processors ("workgroup servers") at a physical location or which run on the LAN servers as described above. Individual workstations and/or terminals will never directly connect to the CAN. These devices will gain access to the CAN only via their LAN connection. In effect, the CAN provides the capability to link multiple LANs together within a physical building and/or across a number of buildings which are in close proximity to each other.

Wide area networks (WANs).

A WAN provides network connectivity between widely dispersed physical work locations, such as between headquarters and field offices. The WAN may be a combination of privately owned network facilities, leased lines, and public network services, such as electronic data interchange (EDI) processing, packet switching, and frame relay, from value added network (VAN) suppliers. A WAN provides the high-speed, long-haul communications links to interconnect the dispersed physical locations of the department. The WAN provides the capability for applications running on LANs and workgroup processors on CANs to communicate with remote site applications. The WAN connectivity also allows access to applications which run centrally on the enterprise processor.

Workstations have access to all networked processors through LAN connectivity

At enterprise and workgroup locations, LANs will not connect directly to the WAN. Instead, they will gain access to the WAN through their connection to the CAN. Likewise, workstations and kiosks will not connect directly to the CAN. Instead, they will gain access to the CAN via their connections to a LAN. Workgroup processors and enterprise processors will connect into the CAN as well. This allows all workstations and terminals to gain access to all processors in XYZ via a standard set of network connections.

To complete the technology view

While the levels of computing and client/server types provide the foundation of the technology view of XYZ's RITA, the technology view is further detailed through a set of associated templates that cross-reference the technology view elements to various elements of the other architectural views (i.e., operations, applications and information).

The templates needed to complete the understanding of the technology view include:

- Target application to level of computing
- Data groups to level of computing
- Target application to client/server implementation type
- Application to GAE affinity matrix

These templates are discussed in detail in the next section of this document. Copies of the completed templates can be found in the deliverables sections.

THE TARGET TEMPLATES USED

A series of templates were used to further detail the architectural renderings previously presented. In the years to come, the templates are intended to provide PMs and implementation teams responsible for implementing this architecture with an understanding of the integration and interdependences among the four architectural models.

Each of the templates used in the target phase of the project is presented and described in the following pages. The completed templates can be found in the deliverables sections. The target templates include:

- Target COGs to current organization matrix
- Target COGs to user class affinity matrix
- Target application to data grouping affinity matrix
- Application characteristics
- Target COGs to target applications
- Target application to target application (integration opportunity)
- Target application to existing application (integration opportunity)
- Target application to user class
- Target application access by physical location
- Target COG to data grouping
- Characteristics of information
- Application to GAE affinity matrix
- Target application to client/server implementation type
- Target application to level of computing
- Data groups to level of computing

Target COGs to Current Organization Matrix

This template, as presented in Figure B.7, cross-references COGs (as presented in the target value chain, discussed earlier) to the current organizational work units making up the department. This view is important for facilitating understanding of which work units currently perform the work intended to be contained in each of the COGs.

Current Organization / Operating Groups	P/L Field Ops	Internal Ops	Claim Financial	Claim HR	Recovery Ops
PLAN					
Perform Business Planning	x				
Manage Budget	x	x	x		
Monitor Policies/Practices	x				
STAFF					
Assign/Manage Work	x	x	x	x	x
Perform Performance Measures					
Provide Personnel Services	x	x	x		
PERFORM					
Manage Loss Reporting	x	x	x		
Investigate/Evaluate Claim	x	x			
Negotiate/Settle Claim	x	x			

Figure B.7   COG to current organization matrix template.

Target COGs to User Class Affinity Matrix

The template cross-references COGs to the types of workers who perform the work represented in the work unit (see Figure B.8). The template clarifies the connection between the generic work to be performed by the department and its worker types.

Target Application to Data Grouping Affinity Matrix

The template in Figure B.9 cross-references the target systems to the data entities that these systems will manipulate (i.e., create, retrieve, modify, and delete). The matrix shows the basic data requirements of each of the target systems envisioned within the department's architecture.

Application Characteristics Template

The template presented in Figure B.10 details the target application systems' needs of the department by quantifying the availability, reliability, and usage requirements of each target system. It also rates each system's contribution to the major business themes that underpin the XYZ vision. This insight will be helpful in prioritizing the target list in subsequent phases of this project.

User Class / Operating Groups	Managers	QA Specialist	Claim Handler	Reserve Specialist	Recovery Staff
PLAN					
Perform Business Planning	x				
Manage Budget	x		x	x	
Monitor Policies/Practices	x	x	x		x
STAFF					
Assign/Manage Work	x	x	x	x	x
Perform Performance Measures	x				
Provide Personnel Services	x				
PERFORM					
Manage Loss Reporting		x	x		
Investigate/Evaluate Claim		x	x	x	x
Negotiate/Settle Claim		x	x		x

Figure B.8 COGs to user class affinity matrix template.

Data Groups / Applications	Insured	Claim History	Account Information	Reserve	Policy
Business Planning System					
Claim Handling System	x	x	x	x	x
Recovery Management System	x	x	x		
Asset Inventory System					
Legal Case System	x	x	x	x	x
Policies DB System	x	x	x	x	x
Performance Measurement System			x		
Customer DB System	x	x	x	x	x
QA System		x	x		x
Vendor Tracking System					
HR System					
Consumer Affairs System	x	x	x	x	x

Figure B.9 Target application to data grouping affinity matrix template.

Applications	Availability	Reliability	Usage Information	Efficiency Contribution	Effective Contribution
Business Planning System	2	1	3	Hi	Hi
Claim Handling System	1	1	1	Hi	Hi
Recovery Management System	2	1	1	Hi	Med
Asset Inventory System	3	3	3	Lo	Lo
Legal Case System	2	2	2	Hi	Med
Policies DB System	1	1	1	Hi	Hi
Performance Measurement System	2	2	2	Lo	Med
Customer DB System	1	1	1	Hi	Hi
QA System	3	2	2	Lo	Hi
Vendor Tracking System	3	2	3	Lo	Hi
HR System	1	1	3	Med	Med

Figure B.10   Application characteristics template.

Target COGs to Target Application Template

This matrix cross-references COGs to the target application systems (see Figure B.11). The template clarifies which work processes use the capability provided by the target applications.

Target Application to Target Application (Integration Opportunities) Template

The matrix in Figure B.12 identifies potential integration opportunities by cross-referencing target applications that share common information and functional components. Project teams responsible for delivering these applications must recognize these common information and functional needs. By doing so, they can capitalize on the integration opportunities they represent and design components for use in each of the target applications which need them.

Target Application to Existing Application (Integration Opportunities) Template

This matrix (as presented in Figure B.13) cross-references target applications to existing applications. It identifies potential integration opportunities between existing and target systems. It does not necessarily recommend this integration, but points the design team toward an existing asset which may be harvested.

Target Application to User Class Template

This template cross-references target applications to the classes of workers who would use them (see Figure B.14). The matrix clarifies who the intended

COGs / Applications	Manage Loss Reporting	Investigate/ Evaluate Claim	Negotiate/ Settle Claim	Establish/ Maintain Reserve	Measure/ Monitor Loss Cost
Business Planning System					X
Claim Handling System	X	X	X	X	X
Recovery Management System		X	X	X	
Asset Inventory System					
Legal Case System		X	X	X	X
Policies DB System	X	X	X	X	X
Performance Measurement System					
Customer DB System	X	X	X	X	X
QA System	X	X	X	X	X
Vendor Tracking System		X	X		
HR System					
Consumer Affairs System	X	X	X		

Figure B.11 Target COGs to target application template.

Applications / Applications	Business Planning System	Claim Handling System	Recovery Management System	Asset Inventory System	Legal Case System
Business Planning System					
Claim Handling System	X		X	X	X
Recovery Management System		X	X	X	
Asset Inventory System					X
Legal Case System		X	X		X
Policies DB System	X	X	X	X	
Performance Measurement System					
Customer DB System	X	X	X	X	X
QA System	X	X	X	X	X
Vendor Tracking System		X	X		
HR System					
Consumer Affairs System	X	X	X		

Figure B.12 Target application to target application (integration opportunity) template.

Applications \ Existing Applications	Automatic Claim System	Data Routing System	Central Management System	Field File System	Legal Matters System
Business Planning System					X
Claim Handling System	X		X	X	X
Recovery Management System		X	X	X	
Asset Inventory System		X			X
Legal Case System					X
Policies DB System	X	X	X	X	
Performance Measurement System			X		
Customer DB System	X	X	X	X	X
QA System	X	X	X	X	X
Vendor Tracking System			X		X
HR System				X	
Consumer Affairs System	X	X	X		X

Figure B.13 Target application to existing application (integration opportunities) template.

application user community will be. It is useful in evaluating the scope of human factor design issues and provides a profile of the user group.

Target Application Access by Physical Location Template

The template found in Figure B.15 cross-references target applications with the physical location from which they will be accessed by workers. In conjunction with other matrices, the matrix provides an indication of network and system administration requirements.

Target COGs to Data Grouping Template

This template cross-references target COGs to data groups, characterizing the basic data requirements of each COGs within the claim department (see Figure B.16). The work processes that the COGs represent create, retrieve, modify, or delete the data entities indicated in the course of their operation.

Characteristics of Information Template

This template (as presented in Figure B.17) details the characteristics of the information needs of the department by characterizing the form, size, speed of access, and currency requirements of each data group. In conjunction with other templates, this insight will be helpful in understanding the demands that will be placed on the network and data management tools and infrastructure.

User Class / Applications	Managers	QA Specialist	Claim Handler	Reserve Staff	Matters Specialist
Business Planning System	X				
Claim Handling System	X		X	X	X
Recovery Management System		X	X	X	X
Asset Inventory System	X	X			
Legal Case System			X	X	X
Policies DB System	X	X	X	X	X
Performance Measurement System	X				
Customer DB System	X	X	X	X	X
QA System	X	X	X	X	X
Vendor Tracking System	X		X		X
HR System	X				
Consumer Affairs System	X	X			

Figure B.14 Target application to user class template.

Physical Location / Applications	HQ	Staff Legal	Ocean Marine	ABCD Staff	Field Locations
Business Planning System	X	X	X	X	X
Claim Handling System	X	X	X		X
Recovery Management System	X	X	X		X
Asset Inventory System	X				X
Legal Case System	X	X			X
Policies DB System	X	X	X	X	X
Performance Measurement System	X	X	X	X	X
Customer DB System	X	X	X	X	X
QA System	X	X	X	X	X
Vendor Tracking System	X	X		X	
HR System	X	X		X	X
Consumer Affairs System	X	X			

Figure B.15 Target application access by physical location template.

Operating Groups \ Data Groups	Insured	Claims History	Account Information	Agency	Policy Information
PLAN					
Perform Business Planning	X			X	X
Manage Budget	X	X	X	X	X
Monitor Policies/Practices	X	X	X	X	X
STAFF					
Assign/Manage Work	X	X	X	X	X
Perform Performance Measures		X	X	X	
Provide Personnel Services	X	X		X	
PERFORM					
Manage Loss Reporting	X	X	X	X	X
Investigate/Evaluate Claim	X	X	X	X	X
Negotiate/Settle Claim	X	X	X	X	X

Figure B.16   Target COGs to data grouping template.

Application to GAE Affinity Matrix Template

This template provides additional details about the probable characteristics of the target applications and identifies the generic technology to be incorporated into the systems targeted (see Figure B.18).

Target Application to Client/Server Implementation Type Template

Client/server environments are characterized by the separation of three elements of the application:

- *Presentation*—what the user sees
- *Function*—the logic of the program
- *Data*—the information stored/retained

These elements of the application may be placed on the client, the server, or both (see Figure B.19 for a breakdown of the options). The template found in Figure B.20, however, categorizes target applications by the type of client/server environment in which they operate.

Target Application to Level of Computing Template

The template presented in Figure B.21 categorizes target applications by the computing level in which they primarily operate. In conjunction with other matrices, this matrix provides an indication of network and system administration requirements.

Characteristics of Data / Data Groups	Information Forms					Volume	Timeliness	Currency
	Character-based	Video	Voice	Image	Document			
PLAN								
Insured	x	x	x	x	x	VL	H	H
Claims History	x	x	x	x	x	VL	H	H
Account Information	x	x	x	x	x	VL	H	H
Agent	x		x		x	L	M	M
Agency	x				x	L	M	M
Policy Information	x	x	x	x	x	VL	H	H
Demographics	x				x	L	L	L
Employee	x	x	x	x	x	L	H	H
Claims	x	x	x	x	x	VL	H	H
Claimant	x	x	x	x	x	VL	H	H
Injury	x	x	x	x	x	VL	H	H
Witness	x	x	x	x	x	M	H	H

Figure B.17 Characteristics of information template.

Applications / Generic Environment	Batch	Transactions Processing	Inquiry	Decision Support	Video Telephony
Business Planning System	X		X	X	
Claim Handling System	X	X	X	X	X
Recovery Management System	X	X	X	X	X
Asset Inventory System	X		X	X	
Legal Case System	X		X	X	X
Policies DB System			X	X	
Performance Measurement System	X		X	X	
Customer DB System	X	X	X	X	X
QA System			X	X	
Vendor Tracking System	X		X	X	
HR System	X		X	X	X
Consumer Affairs System			X	X	

Figure B.18 Application to GAE affinity matrix template.

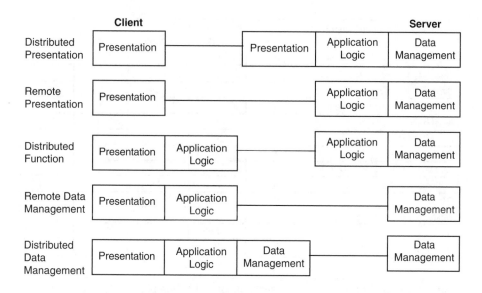

Figure B.19 Client–server implementation types.

Client/Server Type Applications	Distributed Presentation	Remote Presentation	Distributed Function	Distributed Data Management	Remote Management
Business Planning System					X
Claim Handling System	X	X	X	X	X
Recovery Management System	X	X	X	X	X
Asset Inventory System					X
Legal Case System					X
Policies DB System	X				
Performance Measurement System	X				
Customer DB System	X				
QA System	X				
Vendor Tracking System	X				
HR System	X		X		
Consumer Affairs System	X			X	

Figure B.20 Target application to client–server implementation types.

Level of Computing / Applications	Enterprise	Work Group	Individual	Mobile	Remote
Business Planning System	X	X			X
Claim Handling System	X	X	X	X	X
Recovery Management System	X	X	X	X	
Asset Inventory System	X	X			X
Legal Case System	X	X			X
Policies DB System	X	X	X	X	
Performance Measurement System	X				
Customer DB System	X	X	X	X	X
QA System	X	X			
Vendor Tracking System	X	X			
HR System	X	X	X		
Consumer Affairs System	X	X			

Figure B.21   Target application to levels of computing template.

Level of Computing / Data Groups	Enterprise	Work Group	Individual	Mobile	Remote
Insured	X	X	X	X	X
Claims History	X	X	X	X	X
Account Information	X	X	X	X	X
Agent	X	X	X		X
Agency	X	X			X
Policy Information	X	X	X	X	X
Demographics	X	X			
Employee	X	X	X	X	X
Claims	X	X	X	X	X
Claimant	X	X	X	X	X
Injury	X	X	X	X	X
Witness	X	X	X	X	X

Figure B.22   Data groups to levels of computing template.

Data Groups to Level of Computing Template

This template categorizes data groups by the computing level in which they are primarily managed (see Figure B.22). In conjunction with other matrices, this matrix provides an indication of network and data administration requirements.

IN CLOSING

As per the Kerr Consulting Group's IT methodology, the target definition and opportunities phases of the RITA effort were completed in parallel. The projects and programs needed to implement the target RITA presented here are contained in the opportunities identification document.

In a sense, the opportunities identification document can be considered to be a companion piece to this one. Please read that document to better understand how the RITA team sees the target architecture implementation progressing into the future.

With that said, the RITA team will now embark on both the implementation planning and RITA administration phases of the project.

* * *

5

PORTFOLIO-BASED PROJECT MANAGEMENT

Consequently, a new project management mentality materialized within **Your Company, Inc.** *The Company has found that work is best managed as a portfolio of projects and programs, rather than as a set of tasks arranged around a hierarchy of departments—which has become ineffective in overseeing cross-company strategic initiatives as the worker population grows more diverse and transient.*

In the previous chapters, we learned that success in the *Best Practices Era* requires businesses to adopt a new set of approaches for developing both strategic and information technology plans. The methods presented in those chapters outlined the need to organize work into a series of projects and programs.

The fact that *Best Practices Enterprises*™ will be inhabited by a broadly diverse and potentially transient workforce adds a level of complexity to the proposition of managing strategic initiatives as a portfolio of projects and programs. Certainly, inherent communication challenges and the threat of personnel turnover can hurt a firm's ability to execute.

In this chapter, we will explore ways to hedge such risks and manage projects and programs in a well-ordered and purposeful way through portfolio-based project management. It is an important foundational element of the *Best Practices Enterprise*™ (see Figure 5.1).

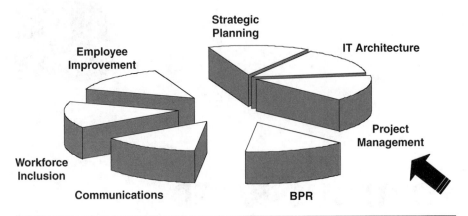

Figure 5.1 Project management is an important element of the foundation.

THE AGE OF FREE AGENCY IS UPON US

They go by many names—consultants, contractors, 1099s, independents, and freelancers. These non-employee workers constitute an estimated 28% of the U.S. labor force.[1] This means that over 30 million Americans are "free agents" who work independently. Their numbers are growing. People like the autonomy that comes with self-employment. Clearly, some of the "best and brightest" prefer it. *Best Practices Era* organizations need to face these facts and plan accordingly.

It should not be too difficult to make the leap. Outdated assumptions about an enterprise's fixed and variable cost structures are being tested. Businesses are beginning to forego size in favor of establishing a more "variable" business enterprise—one that can scale to size and capacity as needed.

Business leaders are seeing that agility beats a behemoth to market every time. This is not to say that large corporations cannot become agile. But, the use of contracted talent is a key ingredient to establishing the needed agility. Hiring *what is needed, when needed* is how the game is won (see St. Peter's Hospital sidebar for an example of this point from the healthcare industry).

But the management and leverage of transitory personnel is not the only challenge facing businesses interested in putting a *portfolio-based project management* process in place. Firms must recognize and develop strategies for overcoming many other obstacles as well.

---

[1]"Nonstandard work, substandard jobs, flexible work arrangements in the U.S.," a white paper published by the Economic Policy Institute and Women's Research and Education Institute, Washington, D.C. and supplemental testimony before the U.S. Department of Labor Working Group on The Benefit Implications of The Growth of a Contingent Workforce by Dr. Edith Rasell, Economic Policy Institute, May 5, 1999.

OTHER OBSTACLES TO CONSIDER

Indeed, a business faces many challenges when establishing a project-oriented culture. After all, change is difficult. Most people do not easily embrace it. In fact, we seem to naturally resist change, regardless of the benefits that it may bring. For most firms, shifting to a project-oriented management structure represents great change. One can expect the resistance to come from many quarters within the enterprise and to manifest itself in many different ways, including:

- Derisory commitment
- Inadequate foundation-setting
- Substandard communication
- Vague portfolio management practices
- Lack of program-centric strategic planning procedures
- Skills deficits

BEST PRACTICES BUSINESS IN ACTION
Leveraging Free Agency at St. Peter's Hospital

Since 2001, St. Peter's Hospital in Albany, New York has been using online shift bidding as a means of leveraging the free agent nursing pool that exists in the area. Since instituting the process, St. Peter's has saved over $1.7 million while lowering its double-digit vacancy rate to less than 5%. The hospital estimates that over 127,000 shift hours have been filled through online bidding.

The bidding process is easy to use. Nurses simply log on to the hospital's website, where they can view all available shifts within the units in which they are qualified to work. From there, the nurses bid on the desired shift by providing their hourly rate. The lowest qualified bidder gets the work.

Interestingly, most work bids-out at approximately 30% higher than the common RN base rate. However, St. Peter's still pays $12 less per hour than it would pay a temporary RN hired through a placement agency. The free agent nurses gain flexibility and independence while the hospital fills needs and saves money.

St. Peter's is not the only hospital using this technique to fill shortages. Other hospitals across the country have followed suit and have enjoyed the same stunning results. Certainly, as *Best Practices Enterprises*™ continue to evolve, other creative ways to harnessing the emerging free agent society will grow in popularity.

Source: Based on "And the winner is...," by Alicia Chang, Associated Press, *The Hartford Courant*, December 22, 2003, p. E1.

Let us briefly discuss each of these to gain a fuller understanding of them. We will describe ways of addressing these challenges later in the chapter.

Derisory Commitment

Cultural change typically comes from the outskirts of society. Certainly, a society's current "winners" have a vested interest in maintaining the status quo. They have gained prominence by playing the current game extremely well. Change the game and these winners may not remain on top. They will resist change.

Therefore, it is no surprise that true commitment to project management practices is very difficult to come by from the upper echelon of many large organizations. However, it is the very lack of proper commitment from the top that inhibits firms from fully realizing the value of project portfolio concepts.

Inadequate Foundation-Setting

Project-oriented implementation efforts will fail without the proper underpinnings. Like any cultural shift, the environment must be conducive to change. Time must be taken to establish the needed frame of references required by staff to grasp the concepts and appreciate the work improvements that portfolio-based practices have to offer.

Insufficient investment in raising awareness, education, and training are sure to lead to missteps and malfunctions. An unwillingness to establish the needed organizational elements (e.g., strategic planning office, portfolio management policies, project management standards, etc.) will doom the implementation effort to failure. Such devices are essential to spearheading widespread involvement and overseeing execution.

Substandard Communication

Poor or deficient communication will cripple the introduction of nearly any type of innovative thinking within an enterprise. Portfolio-based project management is no exception. Early in its implementation, steady communication is needed to demystify project-orientation. As project concepts mature within a firm, standard communication mechanisms must be put into place to keep the process alive.

Plotting the right communication strategy is as important as any other element of portfolio-based project management—without it, implementation efforts will fall short.

Vague Portfolio Management Practices

Once an organization begins to advance project-based concepts, it is important that a distinct set of portfolio management practices be defined and implemented. However, if this is not done, or if the procedures are vague, trouble will ensue.

In most businesses, personnel will seize upon poorly defined operating procedures as an invitation to circumvent the project management process altogether. Portfolio management practices must be clearly articulated and enforced.

Lack of Program-Centric Strategic Planning Procedures

Portfolio-based project management is a natural outgrowth of program-centric strategic planning. An enterprise must embrace the notion of organizing strategic initiatives into projects and programs to give portfolio management concepts a context for understanding. Without this, it is difficult for many firms to make the leap into portfolio-based project management.

Skills Deficits

Project-based skills development becomes the last hurdle to clear once project-oriented concepts take hold within a firm. Without the appropriate skill sets, the portfolio management model will fall flat. It is true that early on staff skills can be augmented through the use of outside experts. However, internal talent must be developed for project orientation to remain vital within the concern.

Among all the challenges discussed above, a skills deficit represents the greatest risk to the long-term success of portfolio-based project management within most companies. Time and money must be invested in building project management competencies or project-oriented work will collapse under its own weight.

With all of these challenges facing *Best Practices Enterprises*™ companies today, how does an organization best prepare itself for implementing portfolio-based project management?

THE PORTFOLIO-BASED PROJECT MANAGEMENT STRUCTURE

There are several essential elements needed to address these challenges and put a portfolio-based project management structure in place within an organization, including:

- Project roles and responsibilities awareness program
- Project identification and project prioritization process
- Project skills development
- Portfolio management and administration

Let us now examine each one of these elements to cement a solid understanding of portfolio-based project management.

Project Roles and Responsibilities Awareness Program

The focus here is to raise awareness of the virtues of portfolio-based project management among management and staff. It is the most direct way in which to address the challenges of derisory commitment and inadequate foundation-setting discussed earlier. The awareness program can be done on a casual basis by developing an informative briefing and going on the lecture circuit within the company—presenting the material to groups of personnel from across the enterprise. More elaborate programs will provide for travel to remote offices. However, teleconferencing and videoconferencing represent less-expensive alternatives.

The executive offices are the first stop of the tour. It is here that their commitment can be garnered. As mentioned earlier, this will be a challenge. But, once given the go ahead to "take the show to the masses," the groundswell of support that will follow may be too much for the management team to resist.

With that said, it is imperative that the briefings are concise and that the project management message is delivered so that it demystifies portfolio-based project management and defines the major roles and responsibilities that the structure brings. The most significant roles include:

- Project manager (PM)
- Project team
- Subject matter expert (SME)
- Project sponsor
- Executive steering committee (ESC)
- Strategic planning office (SPO)

To some this may seem like overkill; however, an organization that is not currently operating under a project-oriented mentality needs to spend time establishing definitions for these roles and educating staff as to their meaning. In many cases, when it comes to introducing project-oriented concepts, it is the only way in which to "win friends and influence people."

Be sure to consider including some of the following thoughts when discussing roles and responsibilities with colleagues:

Project manager

PMs are responsible for leading projects. They oversee the execution of project tasks, manage project budgets and resources, and are ultimately responsible for delivering the results expected from the initiative under their control.

Not everyone makes a good PM. The better ones tend to be well organized, strong communicators, and willing to do whatever it takes to bring their projects in on time and on budget. Charisma is the difference between competent and exceptional PMs. Sometimes it takes some "charm" to motivate people to deliver their best work under challenging circumstances.

Project team

The project team is responsible for performing the work needed to develop the project deliverables (both interim and final) defined in the project plan. They are project staff members, working for the PM, who contribute their time and effort to produce desired results.

While it is true that virtually any staff member can be on a project team, first-rate employees make the best team members. Being punctual, trustworthy, and dependable are traits that easily transfer into a project initiative—regardless of the subject area or project scope.

Subject matter experts

SMEs are business experts possessing specialized knowledge on certain aspects of the business. SMEs provide advice to projects on an "as needed" basis. They ensure that the project teams that they work with gain the information and insight needed to get the job done.

SMEs tend to possess cross-departmental expertise. They are often considered indispensable operationally and for this reason are not assigned full-time project team memberships. In fact, it is common for SMEs to span multiple projects concurrently, allowing them to share knowledge across a multitude of efforts.

Project sponsor

Project sponsors are senior executives responsible for shepherding projects to successful conclusion. They have the duty to assist their project teams in resolving organizational impediments to project success. They work tightly with PMs to ensure a smooth transition from project inception to completion.

In fact, the aim of experienced PMs is to ensure executive involvement throughout their project's life cycle by forging solid relationships with their project's executive sponsors. There is little a PM will not share with her or his project sponsors. In turn, by addressing difficult project issues and concerns as they arise, project sponsors hedge risk and improve outcomes.

Executive steering committee

The ESC is composed of senior management team members and has the responsibility of setting strategic directions and guiding project teams toward results that are appropriate and practical for the company.

Chaired by the president or CEO of the organization, the ESC must demonstrate executive commitment to portfolio-based project management by providing project guidance and assisting in problem resolution when solicited to do so by

BEST PRACTICES BUSINESS IN ACTION

Project Excellence at Achieve Healthcare Technologies

Achieve Healthcare Technologies' 180-person staff provides information systems products and services from its headquarters in Minnesota to over 2500 long-term healthcare facilities nationwide. Using manual project tracking means, the firm was unable to adequately forecast resource needs across its many projects. Productivity suffered.

The management team decided to implement the *Microsoft Office Enterprise Project Management Solution*. It immediately optimized resource allocation, improved project delivery times, and greatly enhanced initiative tracking across its portfolio of projects.

Achieve now believes that it has a comprehensive set of project management tools that are robust enough to support all of its near-future needs. Currently, the tool suite supports over 150 users and tracks 75 active projects. Its integrated time tracking system component is believed to have saved over $50,000 in lost revenue (i.e., time that would not have been properly tracked and billed otherwise).

Clearly worth the investment, Achieve's results speak for themselves. As more *Best Practices Enterprises*™ choose to adopt portfolio-based project management, the thirst for automated tools to support the concepts will grow too—leading to even more sophisticated offerings from the vendor community.

Source: Based on information derived from "Healthcare Company Improves Project Management and Revenue Recognition," www.microsoft.com, 2004.

project sponsors, whom they have charged with marshaling the corporate resources needed for project success.

Strategic planning office

In Chapter 2, we discussed how the SPO is needed to oversee the administration of the program-centric strategic plan. With plan administration as a primary charge, the SPO acts as the conduit between the organization and the senior management team on issues related to project management and execution as well.

Typically working for the chief planning officer (CPO) or other senior manager, the SPO tracks each project effort through regularly scheduled cross-project coordination meetings with PMs. Periodically, SPO staff members meet with the ESC to keep the senior management team abreast of project status—fulfilling an important communication mission within the enterprise.

Defining the roles and responsibilities needed to support a portfolio-based project management structure is simple enough to accomplish. Developing the talent is a greater challenge for most organizations.

Project Skills Development

There are myriad ways of developing project management talent and addressing the skills deficit discussed earlier. The methods fall into two broad categories—top-down and bottom-up. Top-down methods involve the creation and implementation of a comprehensive and integrated training program. Bottom-up methods are grassroots initiatives that tend to evolve and grow over time; talent is developed one project at a time. Both approaches can be effective as long as they are taken up in a focused and deliberate way. Let us examine the two in more detail.

Top-down project management development

Top-down project management development programs are driven from the top of the enterprise. Typically, the human resources or training departments oversees the effort and ensures that the program includes instruction in the gross project skills needed by the organization. They ensure that access to the training opportunities within the program is widely available across the company.

Project skills training will include education in:

- *Project management tools and methodologies*—This type of training consists of both technical and soft skills and covers subjects such as critical path method, project management software, and conflict resolution (see Achieve Healthcare sidebar for an example of the value PM software tools can provide).
- *Project teamwork skills*—This type of training focuses on interpersonal skills and covers topics such as effective communication, valuing individual differences, and advanced listening skills.
- *Project culture orientation*—This type of training helps staff to better understand the cultural changes that the adoption of advanced project management philosophies will impart to an organization. The established ways of acting and communicating, for example, must be shared with internal and temporary staff alike.

Additionally, when outside talent is brought in to work on projects, it is important for the organization to orient these individuals to the norms and expectations of the firm's project practices. In this way, the company can ensure consistency in execution and commonality in communication across projects.

Once a critical mass of personnel is trained and available to work on projects, the SPO can step in and fine-tune project skills through hands-on project coaching. In this way, the firm ensures that staff members are being uniformly trained in gross project skills, while honing proficiencies that are consistent with the organization's corporate culture. See the PM Boot Camp sidebar for an example of a project management office (PMO)[2] driving training for a company.

---

[2]PMO is synonymous with SPO. PMO tends to be used by organizations that do not have a chief planning officer (CPO) and/or strong strategic planning functions in place.

BEST PRACTICES BUSINESS IN ACTION

PM Boot Camp:
You Are in the Project Management Army, Now!

Cultivating project management talent is always difficult. Recently, a client company engaged our firm to help it establish a rigorous project management training course for a dozen of its more aspiring PMs. The resultant "PM Boot Camp," as attendees came to call it, proved to be both challenging and rewarding.

Enlisting the assistance of Padgett-Thompson, we created a 1-week training curriculum in PM tools and techniques that included instruction in subjects such as Gantt, PERT, Microsoft Project, and facilitation skills. A 1-day seminar covering the client's particular PMO procedures and practices was the centerpiece of the offering.

Led by members from both Padgett-Thompson and the client's PMO, the training session was sound. It was well received by the participants. By employing a train-the-trainer model and repackaging the training modules, the firm intends to reoffer the PM Boot Camp in the future.

It is through devising creative techniques such as the PM Boot Camp that *Best Practices Era* enterprises are preparing for the future and working to position for continued success. Clearly, the commitment demonstrated in this example is paying dividends. The client has delivered over 40 projects in the past year and has 36 more on the docket for next year. Surely, more such programs will be springing up in organizations around the globe.

Bottom-up project management development

As the name suggests, bottom-up project management development programs are cultivated from within the lower levels of the organization. Typically motivated from widespread dissatisfaction among the rank and file, bottom-up efforts tend to evolve slowly, one project at a time.

Regardless of pace, the bottom-up technique leverages a disciple model whereby the SPO develops highly skilled project practitioners by working intimately with a specific project team. As knowledge is transferred and skills are developed, past project members are called upon to manage and participate in new project efforts. In time, increasingly more staff members become capable project contributors.

It should be noted that all proper project skills training and orientation, like that outlined earlier, should still be provided when applying the bottom-up method of project skills development. However, because of its grassroots nature, education funding is often limited to that which can be provided to project personnel (both internal and temporary) on a project basis.

Bottom-up project management development efforts tend to take longer to institutionalize than their top-down counterparts, but the changes brought about through bottom-up work often have a longer-lasting effect on the organization. It seems that sponsorship of top-down programs diminishes with executive turnover.

Nonetheless, the results are more important than the means when it comes to investing in projects skills development. *Best Practices Enterprises*™ must develop needed skills in order to realize the benefits of portfolio-based project management.

Project Identification and Priority Setting

As personnel become more comfortable working within a project management culture, new project ideas will come along frequently and from many places within the organization. How does an enterprise determine which ideas are legitimate and worth pursuing? A project identification process must be established. It should include such elements as:

- A process for screening ideas for legitimacy (i.e., the idea is truly a project candidate and not simply a work element or common maintenance task that can be performed within the definition of an existing job title)
- A project opportunity template used to document valid project ideas in a standard way
- A process for formally submitting documented ideas to the senior management team for consideration

While screening techniques can vary, the following can be used test the validity of any new project ideas:

- The idea must be strategic in nature (i.e., the work delivered, or the value acquired, from the initiative contributes to the growth and maturity of the company) *or*
- The initiative will cross departmental boundaries (i.e., requires the effort and participation of more that one department within the company) *and*
- The focus of the initiative is not generally considered a typical work activity that should be performed by a particular business unit *and*
- The effort cannot be classified as an IT maintenance/user support activity

Project ideas that pass muster are then properly documented using a standard project opportunity identification template (see Appendix A for examples).

A project opportunity identification template is a simple form that documents the project's name, describes its intent, outlines the deliverables to be produced, estimates strategic significance, and presents related issues. When completed, the form is submitted to the SPO for inclusion in their strategic planning meetings with the ESC.

Once projects are passed on to the senior management team for consideration, the opportunity is evaluated and its fate is determined. If the effort is deemed to be worthy for inclusion in the firm's strategic plan, it is given a priority and scheduled for execution. At project inception, a detailed project plan for the initiative is developed by the project manager and a team assigned to the effort.

It is important to note that some project details, like task-level time estimates, interim deliverable schedules, and total cost per project, will be developed as part of the detailed project planning that the assigned project manager and team will develop at project initiation. The effort then becomes part of the firm's portfolio of projects to be executed over time.

Portfolio Management and Administration

Much like a fund manager responsible for a portfolio of stocks, the SPO manages the firm's portfolio of projects and programs. Through its work with the steering committee, the SPO helps select projects worth pursuing and identify those initiatives that should be removed from, or given a lower priority within, the strategic plan.

The process involved in managing a portfolio of projects includes:

- Reviewing strategic projects/programs (including plans and budgets)
- Assisting the ESC in adjusting the priorities of the company's strategic initiatives
- Enabling knowledge sharing and work product reuse across projects
- Updating PMs on shifts in corporate project management policies and procedures

As mentioned earlier in the chapter, it is of paramount importance that the SPO build a cross-project coordination procedure into its portfolio administration process. It is the only way for the SPO to keep tabs on the projects as they are being executed (see Jewelers Mutual sidebar for an example).

Scheduled on a monthly basis, project coordination meetings bring all PMs responsible for managing strategic initiatives together with the SPO, creating an environment that fosters project management coaching and promotes cross-project communication, at the same time enabling the SPO to track status.

In turn, the SPO uses the information gathered in these meetings to brief the ESC on the status of the firm's project portfolio. This quarterly review provides top decision-makers within the company an opportunity to review the progress of

BEST PRACTICES BUSINESS IN ACTION

Jewelers Mutual Pays a Toll for Improved Project Management

Jewelers Mutual Insurance Company, Inc. of Neenah, Wisconsin, has been providing insurance and related loss-control services to retail jewelers, wholesalers, and artisans for nearly 100 years. Jewelers Mutual (JM) is known for its high-quality service and dependability throughout the jewelry industry.

In an effort to reign in its many projects and programs, the firm introduced its own version of the project coordination process. In its Tollgate meetings, hosted by the office of the Chief Financial Officer, JM provides a forum for its project leaders to come together weekly to share project status updates and to discuss related issues, risks, and project changes.

In preparation for the meeting, project leaders employ a color-coded technique to create a "dashboard" in which to list their project's milestone dates and deliverables. Items presented in green are trouble free, those in yellow signify risk of breakdown, and those in red indicate project danger points. Indeed, the form is easy to peruse and act upon.

Project problems in need of management resolution are escalated to the senior management team through what is termed the 3M Meeting. Held on the third Monday of every month, the 3M meetings provide senior management with an opportunity to become involved in project direction-setting and problem resolution.

Still in their infancy, the Tollgate/3M meetings are beginning to have a positive impact on the company. Project leaders are feeling more empowered as communication with senior leadership improves, and the work done in these sessions is providing vital input to JM's burgeoning strategic planning process as well.

In the coming year, JM intends to develop the procedural elements needed to formally tie its strategic planning and project management processes tightly together—an important effort for the insurer in its continuing pursuit of *Best Practices* implementation.

key strategic projects/programs while providing an opportunity for the ESC to direct and guide the SPO on the management of the project portfolio.

Following the quarterly review meeting, the SPO updates the strategic plan (as well as any project plans reviewed by the committee) and conveys those changes to the organization through a myriad of communication vehicles.

Communication vehicles will be discussed in more depth in subsequent chapters. For now, it is important to note that effective communication can be quite challenging for an organization to perfect. It is not only an important component of the portfolio management and administration function, but it is a vital part of all of the portfolio-based project management elements discussed above.

With that said, and the fundamentals of *portfolio-based project management* structure defined, let us examine some of the hazards that often snare and entangle organizations attempting to institutionalize advanced project management practices.

COMMON HAZARDS

There are a handful of very common pitfalls that firms must work to avoid when putting forth project portfolio implementation efforts, including these most aptly named hazards:

- The "usual suspect syndrome"
- The "ultimatum approach"
- The "big test" method
- The "land of misfit toys" model
- The "just do it" technique

Let us briefly survey each of these common pitfalls, so that they may be avoided.

The Usual Suspect Syndrome

The usual suspect syndrome is characterized by firms that consistently choose the same personnel to work on every project-related effort, regardless of current workload or other prior commitments.

As the theory goes, staff who make up the usual suspects group within a company are the most productive and reliable resources available. The problems with the theory are that these people often burnout from overwork, other staff members become resentful of these "privileged few," and the organization fails to develop the additional talent that it inevitably needs.

Ultimately, productivity suffers as does the long-term prospects for continued success with portfolio-based project management.

The Ultimatum Approach

The ultimatum approach uses threats and intimidation as a means of motivating personnel to participate in project-related work. While ultimatums may work temporarily, they do not provide the lasting effects that are needed to institutionalize portfolio-based project management.

Organizations should strive to set a tone that encourages staff to become involved in project-oriented work. Compensation models must be established that reward project participation and recognize individuals for their contributions to project success.

The Big Test Method

A distant cousin to the ultimatum approach, the big test method positions project work as a challenge to staff. Personnel are made to believe that they are being "tested" by management when assigned to a project. The thought is that good performance will come from the challenge. While this may happen at some level, once word gets out that the "tests" never end, staff members are likely to become bitter and apathetic.

The Land of Misfit Toys Model

Firms that employ this technique are destined for failure in project-related implementation. In the land of misfit toys model, only those staff members who are deemed expendable by their supervisors and managers are assigned project work. Consequently, project results suffer because project teams are staffed by troublemakers, malcontents, and poor performers of one sort or another. This is certainly no way to run a project or, more importantly, to establish a project-oriented culture.

The Just Do It Technique

Perhaps the most common of the hazards, the just do it technique represents a management mindset that is distinguished by an unwavering desire to complete projects as quickly as possible despite staff resistance and the presence of overlapping priorities.

This type of overzealous attitude can only lead to disaster. Most projects do not lend themselves to rapid delivery, and most staff members cannot keep pace. There are too many balls in the air. A healthier mindset calls for the creation of solid project plans and delivery time tables. It allows the best people available to get the job done.

With these common pitfalls as a backdrop, let us outline the critical success factors needed for achievement in portfolio-based project management.

CRITICAL SUCCESS FACTORS

Among the countless factors that contribute to success in portfolio-based project management, these are the most important ones to consider:

- Cultivate project-oriented staff
- Nurture the SPO
- Provide outside assistance
- Establish common language and procedures
- Build communication infrastructure
- Immerse senior management

- Impose program-centric strategic planning practices

Given below is a brief discourse on each of these success factors.

Cultivate Project-Oriented Staff

Firms must develop the "brain trust" needed to keep project-focused work alive and vital. It is absolutely critical that time and money be invested in developing personnel with the necessary skills. As skill sets mature, a project-oriented culture will emerge. In time, project portfolios will be the way in which work is organized and project execution will be the way work is done.

Nurture the SPO

SPO personnel are the keepers of the project portfolio, and they are the glue that keeps the project management structure together—overseeing execution and coordinating initiatives. It is of great importance that the SPO be fully supported by the senior management team. Its work must be respected across the organiza-

---

BEST PRACTICES BUSINESS IN ACTION

Common Project Language for Belgian Telecom Company

Establishing a common project management language across an enterprise is quite a task. But that is exactly what a Belgian-based telecom operator set out to accomplish. Historically, the organization embarked upon over 70 cross-company initiatives per year. Nearly a thousand of its staff members are called upon to contribute to these efforts. However, many of these projects come in late and over budget. The management team needed to do something because precious resources were being squandered carelessly.

They fashioned three lofty goals for the program:

- Establish a common project management methodology
- Cut time-to-delivery in half
- Deliver all projects on time, on budget, and on scope

Working with Price Waterhouse Coopers, the company embraced the Project Management Institute's *Guide to Project Management Body of Knowledge* as the foundation of its methodology. Through training, piloting, and roll-out, a common project management framework was established within the firm.

Six months into the effort, the goals were being achieved. While it is still early to know if the budget, scope, and delivery objectives can be sustained, it is clear that the organization is well on its way to becoming a "contender" in the *Best Practices Era*.

Source: Based on information derived from "Case study: implementing an enterprise project management methodology based on PMI and best practices," www.pwc.com. 2005.

tion, and every staff member should be made aware of the vital role that the SPO plays within the enterprise.

Provide Outside Assistance

Particularly important early in a company's portfolio management implementation, the use of external expertise helps an organization stabilize its project management efforts while enabling knowledge transfer to internal staff. A firm should seek to jump-start its shift toward project-orientation by garnering outside assistance from people who have "been there, done that."

Establish Common Language and Procedures

Portfolio project management implementation must be deliberately orchestrated. If procedural details are left unattended, chaos will result. Instead, firms must work toward establishing project procedures that will be used universally throughout the concern. In time, a common language will emerge that facilitates communication and speeds understanding (see Belgian Telecom sidebar for an example).

Build Communication Infrastructure

A reliable communication infrastructure is another essential ingredient for success in project portfolio management. Because of differences in project management styles and the personal preferences of the staff involved, a variety of communication tools and techniques are required. Regardless of the medium used, project-related information must be conveyed in a timely and accurate way across the enterprise in order to sustain the portfolio management effort.

Immerse Senior Management

As discussed earlier in the chapter, senior management's commitment is crucial for success. What better way to gain that commitment than through total immersion into the project management process? By involving the executive team in activities such as priority-setting and project sponsorship, their commitment to portfolio management can be gained.

Impose Program-Centric Strategic Planning Practices

Program-centric strategic planning gives portfolio-based project management a framework for understanding. Program-centric practices organize strategic initiatives into projects and programs. A project portfolio is the best technique for managing the projects and programs identified in the plan. Insist on program-centric strategic planning and the need for portfolio-based project management will follow. These two *Best Practices Enterprise*™ concepts are truly symbiotic.

IN CLOSING

As businesses continue to finely hone capabilities for competing in the *Best Practices Era*, the portfolio-based project management concept will take hold. The emergence of the independent workforce, as mentioned at the beginning of the chapter, will certainly serve to fuel interest and refinement in the notion of managing work within a portfolio context.

Indeed, the inevitability of transitory workers, coupled with the other competitive realities outlined in the book, will persist in making portfolio-based project management a way of life within the business world.

Results-focused communications is the subject of the next chapter. It is there that we will examine the importance of conveying the "right" information in the "right" ways to enable success.

* * *

6

UNINTERRUPTED
BUSINESS REDESIGN

Your Business, Inc. has learned how to respond quickly to changes in the marketplace by streamlining operations and business processes through continuous business reengineering activities. With a focus on people, processes, and automated systems, a type of workflow fluidity has been founded that has been unheard of until now. It has refined process redesign so well, in fact, that it can change workflow "on a dime" and introduce new products faster than ever before.

Michael Hammer, the godfather of business reengineering, suggested in his groundbreaking treatise, *Reengineering Work: Don't Automate, Obliterate,*[3] that businesses should raze existing work processes and replace them with new ones that make better use of modern technology. I am not so sure.

While business reengineering is certainly an important business fundamental, it is better practiced thoughtfully than with total annihilation in mind. After all, businesses are comprised of people like you and me. What would I do if someone came along and decided to blow my business unit to kingdom come? Well, depending on my mood, I just might decide to hunker down and return fire!

Obviously, this is not the reaction that most management teams are after when they begin a business reengineering effort. In this chapter, we will look at some ways in which business redesign programs can be executed that will engage and inspire staff to do their best work—and not alienate or put personnel on the defensive (see Figure 6.1).

---

[3]Michael Hammer, "Reengineering work: don't automate, obliterate," *Harvard Business Review*, July–August 1990, pp. 104–112.

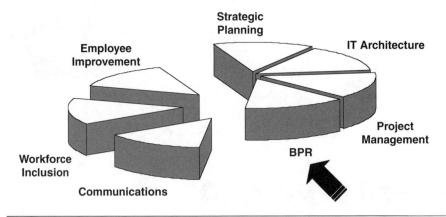

Figure 6.1 Adding business process redesign to the organization.

WHY BOTHER WITH UNINTERRUPTED BUSINESS REDESIGN?

Business reengineering, or *business process redesign* (BPR) as it is often called, is the process of redefining the way work is performed within a business. It explores issues surrounding what work is performed, how it is accomplished, when it is done, and by whom. It is not unusual for a firm to totally reconstruct its workflow and reorganize its workers during a BPR effort (see Nestlé sidebar for more).

Uninterrupted business redesign (U-BPR), on the other hand, takes business reengineering to new heights of relevance by adapting it into an ongoing process that is done continually within organizations as work is performed. This distinction is vital because U-BPR is the only way for business leaders to ready their organizations for the continual transformation required by the competitive environment of the *Best Practices Era.*

With that said, there are several other reasons for firms to seriously consider embracing U-BPR. Firstly, the producer/consumer dynamic has changed. Customers have a broad array of choices. They do not have to accept shoddy quality or service. Alternatives are widely available in the global marketplace of the *Best Practices Enterprise™.*

Secondly, the game has shifted from mass production to mass customization. Manufacturers are recognizing that the only way to keep customers is to deliver to their specifications. Most have embraced quality programs, such as ISO,[4] in

---

[4]ISO is an acronym for the International Organization for Standards. It is a global network that identifies what international standards are required by business, government, and society. ISO then works to develop the standards in partnership with the sectors that will put them to use and adopt them—producing the standards for implementation worldwide.

order to grow and maintain their competitive positions. With the continued advancement of technology, even marketing and advertising have become a one-to-one proposition (see Bimmer sidebar for an example).

The push toward both mass customization and unsurpassed service delivery is leading businesses to become very focused on forging new relationships with vendors who can be entrusted with managing outsourced parts of the business operations—affording firms the ability to scale to size and capacity to meet fluctuating demand.

It is important for companies to consider reengineering business processes now because most business processes were contrived before the advent of the more sophisticated automated support tools that are currently available. While many firms tweak work activities by piling automation on to them, most should redefine their processes before automating them.

Indeed, U-BPR is an essential ingredient in positioning *Best Practices Era* organizations for success in the exciting times that lie ahead. Workflow organization and design need to be continual and ever evolving in order to take advantage of the latest technological advances and to seize market opportunities as they arise.

BEST PRACTICES BUSINESS IN ACTION

One Nestlé: Transformation through BPR

In 2002, as competition brought about through industry mergers and the emergence of retailer private labels began to eat into the food giant's profits, Nestlé USA needed to consolidate its $6.6 billion operation. It turned to BPR to provide part of the solution.

One Nestlé was developed in response to the industry challenges. The program introduced a new vision and strategy for the company, calling for integrating all the U.S. brands under one corporate umbrella and introducing common processes, operating standards, and information systems across the concern.

The multiyear transformation effort is off to a strong start. Supply chain efficiency alone (i.e., order tracking, purchasing, inventory control, etc.) accounts for nearly $325 million in savings since the inception of the One Nestlé initiative.

By redesigning workflows and shifting the way work is done, Nestlé USA has been able to integrate its once disparate operations into a cohesive and more efficient whole. The company is clearly a *Best Practices Era* enterprise—proactively doing what it takes to stay ahead of the competition.

Source: Based on "The right ingredients," www.dc.com/expertise/services/ ent_apps/index.asp, October 10, 2003.

BEST PRACTICES BUSINESS IN ACTION

A Bimmer Just for You

With a focus on one-to-one marketing, BMW is pursuing a personalized direct marketing strategy in the U.S. for its Z4 roadster. Mailings feature the cars in a recipient's favorite color, and the people and setting of the photos reflect the prospective customer's particular demographics as well.

By taking advantage of the latest printing technologies (HP Indigo Press 3000), Redi-Mail of Fairfield, New Jersey, BMW's direct marketing vendor, can customize the 32-page color brochure for each addressee by age, sex, income, and favorite color. The marketing piece is further customized by the inclusion of a personalized note that suggests (from previously gathered information about the recipient) why the person might consider the purchase of the Z4.

While the payback on the investment in this one-to-one marketing effort is still unclear, BMW is expecting to double typical recipient response to the mailing. Nonetheless, this technique of speaking to potential customers as individuals and creating personalized direct marketing to targeted individuals is a *Best Practices Era* practice that is sure to catch on as consumers' sophistication continues to grow and their demands continue to become more discerning.

Source: Based on "HP Indigo Press 3000 provides BMW with personalized direct marketing campaigns," www.h30046.www3.hp.com/casestudy, October 8, 2003.

Global integration, customized products/service offerings, and ultra-responsiveness are the goals shared by every *Best Practices Era* business. By implementing U-BPR today, firms improve their chances of achieving these goals tomorrow.

THE KEYS TO U-BPR

Change is always difficult to implement, and the scale of change that U-BPR effort imposes on the work environment can be quite dramatic for everyone involved. When U-BPR is fully institutionalized within a firm, it will have become an important element of the company's culture and will inform its work setting for evermore. After all, success is about creating an environment of continual rebirth within the enterprise (see Cummins sidebar for an example of a firm that has embraced the concept).

For this reason, a rigorous BPR method must be adopted when first doing the work needed to jump-start U-BPR. The methodology chosen must be straightforward and able to deliver quick and lasting results. The key characteristics of a worthy jump-start approach include provisions for:

- Building the "right" *team*
- Establishing the "right" *setting*
- Conducting thorough *business modeling*
- Performing thorough *process analysis*
- Redefining the *value chain*
- Creating necessary *transition plans*

Let us examine these elements in more detail.

Building the "Right" Team

The project team is possibly the single most important determinant of success in a U-BPR effort. There are several roles that must be played, and played well, for the project to have any hope of having a lasting effect on the business.

The team must be led by an experienced BPR facilitator. The work cannot be done by simply reading about how to do it in a book. Experience does count here. Someone who has done their time in the trenches and can anticipate the trials and tribulations that are typical in a BPR engagement is required.

BEST PRACTICES BUSINESS IN ACTION
Uninterrupted BPR at Cummins

Cummins is a designer and manufacturer of high-performance diesel engines and electrical power generation systems. Headquartered in Columbus, Indiana, the firm has operations all over the world.

A few years ago, Cummins embraced the notion of continuous process improvement. It chose to implement Six Sigma Statistical Analysis as the underpinning of its U-BPR methodology. While Six Sigma has a heavy statistical analysis bent, seeking to measure process inputs and outputs and documenting variances as a means for determining actions for change, it does provide the measurement tools needed to assist firms in discovering process improvement opportunities.

Clearly committed to changing the culture and establishing a new way of doing business, Cummins has trained thousands of its staff members in the Six Sigma methodology. Over 1000 Six Sigma projects have been completed worldwide. The company has achieved almost $400 million in corporate savings through the efforts—a clear indication that the process is working.

The Cummins example is proof positive that U-BPR is a *Best Practices Era* stalwart that cannot be ignored.

Source: Based on "Using Six Sigma Statistical Thinking to improve business processes," www.tt100.biz, 2004.

While a strong facilitator is a key to success, surrounding the leader with some strong players is also extremely important. These players can be classified into three broad categories that we will call *gofers*, *grunts*, and *analysts*.

Gofers are people from the business area who can seek and retrieve important information about the business that is needed by the team to do its job. Because they are from the business area, they know where to find items like sample work documents, policy and procedure manuals, and job descriptions.

Grunts are usually consultants, but they can also come from the business. These individuals put together all the work products and recommendations that will be delivered. Not to be confused with clerical assistants, the grunts grind out content. They must be skilled at writing thorough business reports and preparing convincing management presentations.

Analysts study organizations. Specifically, they study the way work is done by businesses and try to identify better ways of doing it. Like the grunts, they can come from either the business or the consulting ranks. Objectivity and business experience are the keys to their effectiveness.

Keep in mind that the BPR team does not have to be large. In fact, a four- or five-person team tends to be most effective. But the best BPR teams have a sprinkling of all types of talent. When a team is lucky, some of its members are strong enough to play more than one role.

Establishing the "Right" Setting

Business reengineering work is a combination of fact gathering, synthesis, and analysis. Fact gathering is best done in a workshop setting where information can be freely expressed and supplemental opinions can be sought from the business experts in attendance. Synthesis and analysis, on the other hand, are best done by the BPR team in private—where issues can be discussed and conclusions drawn without interference by concerned parties not specifically on the team.

With that said, it is recommended that a BPR project room be established that can be used exclusively by the BPR team. It should be large enough for conducting workshops with other business people, have plenty of wall space for posting information gathered in workshops, and provide personal work space for each member of the BPR team.

Because this "war room" will be a team member's home away from home, basic office equipment (e.g., telephones, personal computers, printers, and fax machines) should be available for use by each member. Access to copying machines, office supplies, and administrative support is also important, especially during "crunch time," when team members are busy producing the final deliverables.

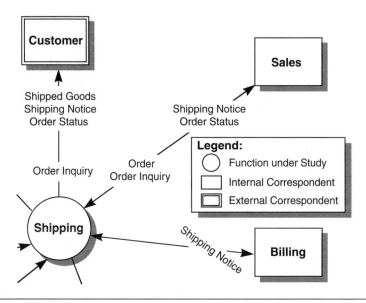

Figure 6.2 Sample business model diagram.

Business Modeling

Business modeling is a technique for defining the boundary and scope of a business reengineering effort. Its aim is to determine the workflow within each business area within the enterprise and to discover both the internal and external correspondents with which each business area interacts in the course of executing its basic mission.

A business model diagram, such as the one in Figure 6.2, is built for every functional area, and it reflects this information. These models are built in the workshop by the BPR team and subject matter experts from the business community.

As can be seen in our example, the business function being reengineered sits in the middle of the diagram, and the internal and external business correspondents are represented along the periphery. The workflow is defined as the flow of information between the business area and its correspondents.

Additional information about the business area, such as throughput volumes, production statistics, process triggers, and average turnaround times, can also be captured as the diagram is being developed. This data will provide valuable insight into the inner workings of the business areas constituting the firm and will help the team determine how to best begin its U-BPR effort of introducing continual workflow redesign within the enterprise.

Process Analysis

The heart of any BPR methodology is its approach to analyzing the business processes that underpin the business. The final BPR change recommendations are only as good as the project team's ability to discern the facts about the way work is performed and what can be done to improve it. Therefore, the process analysis approach has to be solid for the subsequent U-BPR effort to be worth anything at all.

Process analysis begins by reviewing the business models that were created earlier in the launch effort. The project team, in essence, tries to poke holes in the model and identify alternative ways of getting the job done. It reviews the facts and statistics gathered and distinguishes weak points and improvement areas within each of the business models.

Frustration can set in without an organized way to go about this type of analysis. Much pain and heartache can be avoided by applying a predetermined and integrated set of questions concerning *who, what, where, when, why,* and *how.* It is through appropriate examination that breakthrough improvement opportunities can be identified for the business (see WellPoint sidebar for an example of how solid analysis can pay off).

A project team can quickly draw conclusions about the status of a particular business process by exploring questions such as:

- Who does it today?
- Who else could do it?
- Who should do it?
- When is it done?
- When could it be done?
- When should it be done?
- Where is it done?
- Where could it be done?
- Where should it be done?

The process analysis approach used can and should include 70 to 80 such questions. A dialogue focused on these questions can lead to additional ones focused on work material, personnel, and measurement practices.

With the answers to these kinds of questions in tow, the BPR team can begin to consider alternative ways of designing the workflow and organization of the business. Experience has shown that a value chain depiction is the best way for a team to present its initial recommendations for change.

The Value Chain

A value chain is a graphical representation of all the work that must be done by a business or work area in order to provide its goods/services (i.e., "value") to its cus-

BEST PRACTICES BUSINESS IN ACTION

Attacking Claims Leakage at WellPoint

WellPoint was clearly overpaying its health claims and needed help. It began a major BPR initiative aimed at looking for ways of streamlining the claims handling process and achieving the cost savings that the management team knew existed.

The overpayment of health claims (known as "leakage") is a major challenge for most insurers, routinely accounting for millions of dollars in inappropriate claims. Factors such as these highlight the problem:

- Duplicate submissions
- Payment of uncovered charges
- Lack of benefits coordination
- Inaccuracy in contract usage

Making up nearly 85% of the cost structure, inappropriate claims have a direct impact on gross margin and profitability.

The BPR effort conducted within the California division of WellPoint was able to determine its major causes of leakage, to identify cost-effective solutions to overcome the problems, and to develop a multiyear plan of attack to remedy the situation.

Through a combination of automation and process improvements, the firm has been able to reduce claim leakage by $65 million. The WellPoint experience exemplifies how a well-directed BPR initiative can pay dividends. It serves as living proof of another *Best Practices Era* business seeking ways of cost-effectively competing in a highly competitive marketplace, where margins are tight and costs are a determining factor for success.

Source: Based on "Case study: WellPoint," www.accenture.com, 2003.

tomers. It is a valuable means of presenting a normalized view of the business. It is free from redundancies and non-value added work activities. An observer can clearly see how work activities can be strung together to forge a new, high-quality process design.

A value chain should be built for each business area. These models are valuable for presenting new and different ways of thinking about an enterprise. Because value chains are independent of existing organizational structures, staff, and work locations, they are less intimidating to the management and staff who have a vested interest in the *status quo*. These players are less likely to resist any recommendations for dramatic change in their area of the business, if it comes in an objective, non-threatening way (see Bangkok Bank sidebar for an example of how BPR work can redefine the way a business is organized).

Value chains are comprised of conceptual operations groups (COGs). COGs are generic bundles of work, which have been stripped free from any association to the current work environment. Like the cogs in a machine, these COGs make

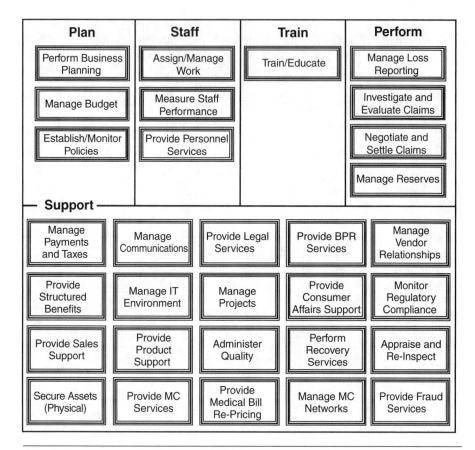

Figure 6.3 Sample value chain diagram.

the value chain work. In fact, we can think of a value chain as really just a network of COGs (see Figure 6.3).

As shown in Figure 6.3, a value chain is organized into five components or categories. All the work performed by any organization can be grouped into these five basic categories:

- *Plan*, which contains a collection of COGs that support the planning activities within a business area
- *Staff*, which contains a collection of COGs that support staffing activities within a business area
- *Train*, which contains a collection of COGs that support training activities within a business area
- *Perform*, which contains a collection of COGs that support the core work activities within a business area

- *Support*, which contains a collection of COGs that are performed in the support of all the other COGs in the value chain

Figure 6.3 presents a sample from the claims department of a major insurance company. Note that the COGs have no reference to the typical functional areas or business units that one would find in a claims department and that no chain-of-command can be inferred from the value chain's depiction of claims processing.

What is not readily perceptible from Figure 6.3 is that this value chain represents a major departure from the way the company originally viewed its claim handling function. The BPR effort that was performed there made the department's staff "think out of the box" and truly redefine itself—which is what U-BPR is all about.

Once the value chains are defined for a business, all the COGs are thoroughly documented. The format includes a brief description of the COG, a high-level event model that depicts the workflow within the COG, and separate discussions of the related people, processes, and technology issues that underpin the COG (for a more in-depth example, see Appendix C).

Once fully documented, the value chain represents the BPR team's recommended work environment. All that is left to do is develop the plans for the projects that are needed to actualize this target work setting and institute a process for continual change (E-BPR).

Transition Planning

It is not unusual for hundreds of issues to be uncovered and documented through the value chain development effort. These issues are then synthesized and translated into new project initiatives for the company. It is through the execution of the identified projects that U-BPR really takes hold within an organization.

It is imperative that the BPR methodology adopted have a strong transition planning component within it. This way, the BPR team will be sure to convert the open issues it has identified into actionable items through the creation of detailed project plans.

The project planning template presented earlier in the book should be employed in the development of each individual project plan. The template provides a standard way of developing the project plans and renders a common method for defining the intended outcome of each project.

Once the project plans are crafted, they should be prioritized and grouped into implementation plateaus (see Chapter 2 for a detailed explanation of these ideas) to form the finalized U-BPR implementation plan. The resultant U-BPR implementation plan should then be incorporated into the firm's program-centric strategic plan.

In this way, the organization is able to see where its U-BPR initiatives "fit" within the larger context of all the enterprise's planned projects. This ensures that

BEST PRACTICES BUSINESS IN ACTION

Rebuilding Bangkok Bank through BPR

Bangkok Bank is the largest bank in Thailand and one of the largest in Southeast Asia. With foreign competitors such as Citibank and Standard Chartered eating up the local competition, the bank has to stay alert and focused.

In 2001, the concern embarked upon an ambitious business redesign program. Its focus was to realign Bangkok Bank's entire branch structure—reorganizing its 500 branches and introducing a shared-services model to reduce costs and enhance its purchasing power.

In just 3 years, the bank was able to:

- Restructure around customer segments, providing ways of delivering better service and enhancing customer loyalty.
- Place focus on sales and services (and away from the simple transaction-processing mentality that was in place previously), improving revenue and profitability.
- Introduce performance scoring as a means of transforming the culture toward results-focused measurement.

By doing so, Bangkok Bank's stock price rose over 23%, loan growth exceeded that of its competition, and the concern returned to profitability for the first time since the Asia financial crisis of the late 1990s—a certain indication that U-BPR work is worth the investment for today's *Best Practices Era* organization.

Source: Based on "Bangkok Bank," *Booz Allen Hamilton Magazine*, Spring 2004, pp. 33–34.

the senior management team is positioned to make informed decisions about where the organization should invest its time and money.

HOW TO MAKE IT STICK

Once armed with a dependable U-BPR approach, an enterprise must set about incorporating the use of the method into the very core of its strategic thinking, for it is through business reengineering that an organization is transformed. U-BPR provides the means for a business to reinvent itself—something that businesses will need to do in order to compete in the *Best Practices Enterprise*™ world. Let us probe the rudiments of U-BPR execution.

Embrace the Philosophy

First, we need to raise everyone's awareness of what U-BPR is all about. This can be done in myriad ways using some combination of training and the deliberate use of the communication devices described in the next chapter.

Regardless of the methods employed, the focus of the message should be that U-BPR is not a choice, but a matter of survival. Stress the fact that companies that are actively changing and improving will always fare better than those that are complacent and locked into existing work paradigms.

Put People Behind It

Next, management teams must put money where their mouths are. A BPR-specific function should be established and staffed by a team that knows how to provide U-BPR services. Most firms go out to the marketplace and recruit consultants to join the company to drive the creation and management of the function. However, the new group can be formed around experienced employees as well.

Nonetheless, by putting people behind it, we send a clear message that the company is serious about U-BPR work and that it is willing to do whatever it takes to gain the skills to do it right. Secondly, by making U-BPR someone's full-time job, the company is ensuring that the U-BPR process will get the attention it needs to be successfully executed. It really cannot be done to the extent described here on a part-time basis.

Make It a Standard Practice

Once the organization is positioned to deliver the necessary U-BPR services, it is time to require that redesign work be done. An effective way of jump-starting this notion is to begin the work by adopting a business principle that requires every new automation effort to be preceded by a BPR project.

New automation projects always include some form of fact gathering about the business requirements for the new system. A BPR effort done at this point in a project could yield far-reaching results for the business and will certainly shed additional light on the automation needs of the enterprise.

Further, it makes sense to do a BPR review when:

- Introducing new products/services to the marketplace
- Considering strategic options such as outsourcing, commercializing internal departments, and mergers/acquisitions
- Reorganizing departments within the company

Showcase Results

Lastly, we must promote the value of BPR work across the enterprise. This can be done easily through the proper leveraging of existing communication vehicles. How successes are promoted is not as important as ensuring that they are promoted. Just do it!

Remember that people's reactions to, and acceptance of, wholesale change will follow a typical bell curve. Some staff members will embrace it immediately; some will resist it as long as possible. Most, however, will wait and see if the company is truly committed to the change. By showcasing results as they are gained, a firm helps the staff caught in the middle of the curve to jump on board sooner than they might otherwise. With some luck, businesses may even win over some of the detractors.

IN CLOSING

U-BPR work is never done. Instead, an enterprise that is committed to continuous business reengineering is truly a work in progress. With a BPR program in place, these organizations are constantly evolving and changing in new and exciting ways. A BPR culture emerges, and quality and improvement in all that is done become important company values.

So, to close, let us not annihilate. There is a better, more thoughtful way to go about business reengineering that still provides the gains that are needed and positions tomorrow's *Best Practices Enterprises*™ to seize the moment as opportunities arise.

* * *

 Web Added Value™

This book has free material available from download from the
Web Added Value™ resource center at *www.jrosspub.com*

SAMPLE VALUE CHAIN CASE STUDY

DEFINING THE "COGS" IN THE VALUE CHAIN

Conceptual operations groups (COGs) are the logical groupings of work activities that make up a reengineered business or business area. They are represented in a value chain such as the one in Figure C.1. The COGs must be fully documented so that management and staff within the organization can completely grasp the changes recommended by the BPR team.

At a minimum, each COG definition should contain the following:

- A COG description
- An event model, depicting the workflow within the COG
- A discussion of related people issues
- A discussion of related process issues
- A discussion of related technology issues

Derived from an actual BPR effort conducted within a claims operation at a major insurance company, the following exemplifies what might be found in the "manage loss reporting" COG.

Loss Reporting

Description

This COG provides for those services required to capture loss-related information. It encompasses the activities involved in receiving notice of loss from various sources, including agent(s), insured(s), claimant(s), or other carrier(s),

Event Model Diagram

Figure C.1   Event model excerpt.

recording the initial loss-specific information, assigning values to information gathered (coding), and assignment to claim specialists for adjudication.

Once a loss is reported and data are gathered to establish a claim record, decisions are made regarding the appropriate resources required for handling the claim. Claim assignment to a loss team member(s) (claim handlers, appraisers, care managers, vendors, etc.) is accomplished via the assign/manage work COG. Contacts are made with the insured/claimant to acknowledge receipt of the loss and/or provide further instruction.

If a loss is reported by a party other than the insured or an agent, verification is made to determine if a loss event has actually occurred.

As can be imagined, there are many issues and implications that result when embracing this new way of thinking about the loss-reporting process in an insurance company. These issues can be categorized as people issues, process issues, and technology issues (see the following examples).

People issues

1. Highly skilled claim handlers may receive initial loss information: *a culture change for handlers.*
2. Loss-reporting personnel may be the primary claim handlers: *enabling loss reporting direct-to-handler on all claims, in all lines.*
3. Advanced computer skills are needed: *a person using a graphical user interface (GUI), who is comfortable with a mouse, can traverse the system quickly.*
4. Customer support skills are required: *personable, polite, empathetic, thorough approach.*
5. Personnel with multilingual skills may be required: *helps to support customers and retain growth.*
6. New kinds of training will be required: *on-demand, self-paced, PC-based.*

Process issues

1. Operation is $24 \times 7 \times 365$.
2. Operation could be centralized for economies of scale and ease of management.
3. Process is front-ended by moving investigation work forward into the loss-reporting process.
4. All loss-reporting conversations can conclude with a summarization of next steps and the dissemination of handling team information to claimant: *names and numbers of staff assigned to case.*
5. File strategy considerations begin at time of loss report when claim severity and complexity can be determined.
6. Concierge service could be offered to third-party claimants: *sell new policies by providing great service.*

Technology issues

1. Acceptance of multimedia loss reports: *Internet, fax, voice, smart card*
2. Access to customer information at time of report: *products, coverage, special instructions*
3. Use of electronic scripts for data capture process: *standard automated checklists and pick lists for quick loss reporting*
4. Attachment of scanned images to claim file
5. Attachment of audio/video clips to claim file

Note: Each COG receives this kind of treatment.

IN SUMMARY

Literally hundreds of issues related to the reengineered business area are documented this way. As can be imagined, these issues easily translate into new project initiatives for the company. It is through the execution of the identified projects that reengineering is achieved.

In the case of this client, nearly four dozen new initiatives emerged. The business area studied continues its *Best Practices Enterprise*™ evolution to this day.

* * *

Web
Added
Value™

This book has free material available from download from the
Web Added Value™ resource center at *www.jrosspub.com*

RESULTS-FOCUSED COMMUNICATIONS

A focus on business communication has emerged as well. Solid communication vehicles have been put into place to ensure that everyone involved in any way with the business is kept abreast of what is going on and has access to everyone in the firm. It is the only way to ensure that **Your Business, Inc.** *is leveraging all its resources to the fullest.*

This chapter focuses on a results-focused communications program. As Figure 7.1 suggests, this program provides the communication element of the pie. Communicating relevant information to all with "a need to know" is the single most important thing a company can do: it builds trust among employees; gains the confidence of the investment community; and establishes solid relationships with customers and suppliers and all other stakeholders. However, communicating relevant information to all with a need to know is extremely difficult to accomplish.

Why? Because most management teams believe they already do a fine job of communicating. After all, senior leaders make a point of ensuring that elaborate memoranda go out announcing all of the important stuff:

Worker:	*"Hey, you going to the Christmas party?"*
Coworker:	*"What Christmas party?"*
Worker:	*"You know, the office party. It was in that memo we got last week."*
Coworker:	*"Oh, yeah. Uhmm …"*

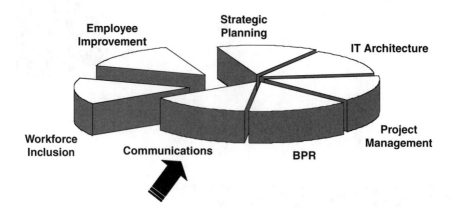

Figure 7.1 Filling in the communications piece.

And, let us not forget the annual meetings. Every year company personnel are gathered together (sometimes in an exotic locale, sometimes not) and, reminiscent of a high school pep rally, they are told by the chief executive how good the company is and how it is going to "crush" the competition next year.

Executive: *"Now, that is communications!"*
Unsuspecting management consultant: *"It sure is!"*

We must become more purposeful about corporate communications. Businesses are just doing a poor job at it. Consider a recent survey conducted by Chicago-based International Survey Research in which 16,000 workers at 104 U.S. businesses were polled to determine common corporate communication habits and practices. It was found that 63% of respondents hear about important business matters through rumors, gossip, and other informal sources.[5] Shocking!

Ultimately, organizations that are serious about improving results must establish a program deliberately aimed at managing corporate communications, providing consistent and reliable means for conveying vital business information through:

- Interoffice communications
- Education and training
- Industry and financial news
- Executive communications
- Crisis communications

---

[5]Carol Kleiman, "Workers learning too little from boss," *The Harford Courant*, September 12, 2005, p. 1E.

- Community access broadcasting
- Motivation and staff recognition
- Brand reinforcement

A RESULTS-FOCUSED COMMUNICATIONS PROGRAM

A results-focused communication program is intended to establish a set of processes and the supporting communication vehicles that impart information to a company's staff and all of its stakeholders, including customers, suppliers, distributors, and stockholders. The focus of such a program is results. It is not enough to establish ways for staff to communicate if the information communicated does not deliver value to the business. An effective communications program provides a reliable mechanism for getting things done.

As mentioned earlier in the book, the age of the *Best Practices Enterprise*™ will bring about the true globalization of business. Many of today's senior business leaders manage their organizations internationally. They view each location as a remote office that is separate and distinct from the firm's other operations in the world. To manage the enterprise "*globally*" is a different management paradigm. It requires the management team to think differently about the essence of the business. The company is no longer thought of as having separate and distinct entities. It is a web of interdependent parts that spans the globe—independent of physical location. Dependable communications frameworks are a "must have" in supporting this type of emerging location independence.

Furthermore, staff inclusion is an essential element of morale. Good morale is needed for achieving strong business results. Communication projects aimed at specific special interest groups can also emerge (e.g., union workers, minority staff, disabled employees). These types of efforts are an important part of a corporate communications plan. They contribute to the well-being of the enterprise (see State of the Union sidebar for more insight).

Once the communications processes are established and the communications vehicles needed to transport and convey the information are in place, personnel are then instructed in how to use them properly and encouraged to fold communication work steps into all that they do—fostering communications across the concern.

With perseverance, communications can become the lifeblood of the company. Let us look at the work involved in getting this important *Best Practices Era* program off the ground.

BEST PRACTICES BUSINESS IN ACTION

State of the Union

The state of Connecticut's Department of Revenue Services (DRS) is responsible for collecting the taxes due the state. There are over two dozen different tax types in the state's tax code that the agency is responsible for collecting. Larger than most other state agencies, the Tax Department employs nearly a thousand auditors, tax clerks, attorneys, and administrative personnel. About 70% are members of collective bargaining units.

As it is with many large organizations, communications was a "trouble spot" within DRS. Important agency news and communiqués were not provided to employees consistently or in a standard way, sometimes leading to misunderstanding and confusion.

Initially hired to develop the strategic plan for the agency, my firm had to quickly gain perspective on the organization. It was apparent that better communication mechanisms needed to be established between the Managers' Advisory Committee (as the senior management team is known at the agency) and the union chiefs that represented the staff.

Union leadership was aggressively resisting the changes that DRS needed to make regarding the way work would be done and the way positions would be staffed. A Union Awareness Project was introduced through the agency's strategic plan. Its aim was to improve the communication links between the agency and the unions.

A cross-agency communication task force was established to drive the awareness effort. The group formalized the use of briefings, memos, and newsletters to provide union leadership with the details of all proposed changes in a timely, accurate, and productive way. More importantly, it chartered an ongoing union communication committee, consisting of management and staff, to provide a regularly scheduled opportunity for the parties to engage in meaningful dialogue and exchange ideas for improving agency operations.

Thus far, the results have been good:

- Union leadership has a better understanding of the pressures that the agency faces.
- Agency management has a better grasp of union issues.
- Agency staff members recognize the value of working together in good faith to arrive at the best approaches for implementing the changes that will make the agency a better place to work.

Communication projects aimed at special interest groups such as this one in Connecticut do work. We need to recognize their importance and be willing to make the effort required for their success. Put simply, it is what every *Best Practices Enterprise*™ must be willing to do to harness the power of a diverse workforce!

GETTING RESULTS-FOCUSED COMMUNICATIONS OFF THE GROUND

There are several steps that an organization must take to establish a communications program that will stand the test of time. They include:

Making It a Project

Like the other fundamental business strategies discussed in the book, the construction of a communications program requires full-time commitment. A firm cannot expect to put together a meaningful communication strategy "on the fly." There are simply too many issues to consider, including:

1. Making the process of establishing the communications program a project
2. Naming an executive from the steering committee to sponsor the effort
3. Assigning a project manager to oversee day-to-day activities
4. Forming a small team to do the "leg work"
5. Disbanding the team once their program recommendations have been accepted by the ESC

Weaving these elements into a formal initiative, one that is properly staffed, funded, and overseen, positions the communications program to become a meaningful element of the *Best Practices Enterprise*™.

Conducting a Stakeholder Assessment

A stakeholder assessment of current company communications practices should be conducted some time early in the project. A good cross-section of suppliers, distributors, customers, and internal staff should be tapped to get their impressions about the frequency, quality, effectiveness, and variety of communications employed by the organization.

By gaining stakeholder perspectives, the project team is positioned to quickly understand the issues at hand. This will give it a running start toward identifying improvement strategies.

Establishing a Baseline

Once the stakeholders are polled, a baseline of the current communications within the enterprise should be established. It is important for the project team to know what devices are already in place. They can then determine which ones work well, and should be used in the future, and which ones need improving.

In all likelihood, some of the existing communication devices will be combined to form more effective ones, while others will be retired and replaced by

BEST PRACTICES BUSINESS IN ACTION

...And, Now, A Message From Ford

The Ford Communications Network (or FCN, as it is known at Ford) was formed in the early 1980s, when the company was going through some tough times and was always in the national news. Rather than having its employees receive information about lay-offs and losses from network newscasts, Ford's management team decided to break it to them themselves.

With some people "moonlighting" from local news stations, Ford put together an experienced staff of producers, directors, reporters, and camera crews to pump out high-quality news telecasts from its newsroom at corporate headquarters. Today, FCN's daily news programs reach over a quarter million employees worldwide at Ford factories and offices.

FCN is used by the automaker to broadcast relevant industry and financial news, employee recognition information, executive messages, and crisis communiqués, as well as special interest stories about staff from around the company.

The firm even conducts its own version of the Academy Awards—the Communicator's User Conference. It is an opportunity for the over 100 program editors, representing Ford sites around the globe, to get together and compare notes and share insights on how to better use the medium to communicate within the company.

This kind of commitment to corporate communications is a clear indication that results-oriented communications programs can have deep roots and staying power. Ford's early work in this area provides the foundation for improving company performance well into the *Best Practices Era*.

Source: Based on information provided on the website: www.targetvision.com, October 6, 2001.

new ones. The baseline effort helps to outline some of the options available to the firm.

Defining a Bull's Eye

A target communications environment should be defined next. The recommendation should include details such as:

- An overview of the types of communications available (i.e., phone, fax, e-mail, memos, intranet)
- Advice on when and how each type should be used
- The regularity with which certain types of communications should be delivered to, or solicited from, specific stakeholder types
- A roll-out plan that describes how to implement the program within the company

Although the implementation responsibility is not necessarily that of the original project team, it is always an option to keep the team in place until the communication program is fully realized. A better scenario is to appoint a PM to oversee the communication program's roll-out. This way, the person closest to the details will assume the role of institutionalizing the program—centralizing project accountability while improving the probability of its ongoing success.

COMMUNICATION VEHICLES

Regardless of who is given the implementation responsibility for the communications program, the person or team will spend a fair amount of time ensuring that a set of effective communication vehicles is put in place to transport company communications to, from, and within the stakeholder community.

Ford Motor Company, for example, went so far as to establish its own television network to manage corporate communications (see Ford sidebar for more). Most organizations would not go to that extent. However, developing a suite of communication devices and defining how and when they are used is an essential *Best Practices Enterprise™* activity.

The graphic in Figure 7.2 suggests some of the more popular communication vehicles used by businesses today.

Figure 7.2 Some important communication vehicles.

These are only a few communication vehicles that can be used. But together, they form the foundation for a solid communications program. Let us explore each of these mechanisms in more detail.

Status Reports

Status reporting is a primary communications vehicle within most businesses. Status reports are one of the easiest ways for a project team to describe where it is in its project plan. The reports can also be used to document issues related to project delays and *scope creep* so that the management team and business planners can help address them proactively.

Status reporting will continue to play an important role within a firm's communications program in the *Best Practices Era*. How it is performed will certainly change and be enhanced. Standardizing reporting formats and structures, integrating composition tools with project management packages, and automating reporting and distributing are already in use today. These will continue to evolve.

In fact, in an interesting twist, Johns Hopkins Hospital is using this type of communication vehicle to improve the quality of critical care within its intensive care unit. See the Johns Hopkins sidebar for more.

Quality Reviews

A quality review process should be established that can be applied to every project as it evolves through its project plan. This "process check" provides an opportunity for project teams and business planners to discuss project status and discover better ways of getting things done.

Figure 7.3 outlines the steps that make up a typical quality review process. According to W. Edwards Deming,[6] the quality pioneer, a project is planned, work begins, the result is checked against the plan, and opportunities for improvements are defined and acted upon through modifications to the plan. Most modern quality programs are based on Deming's theory.

The use of this technique, or one like it, will help a firm to continuously improve on what it is doing. It provides PMs with a trouble-free way of discussing status and communicating changes in project direction.

Lessons Learned Chronicle

Often overlooked, documenting the "lessons learned" (see Figure 7.4) from every project initiative embarked upon by a firm can become very valuable. It helps future PMs in the company to "never make the same mistake twice." It enables

---

[6]W.E. Deming, *Out of the Crisis*, MIT Center for Advanced Engineering Study, Cambridge, MA, 1982.

BEST PRACTICES BUSINESS IN ACTION

Clear Communications at Johns Hopkins

A couple of years ago, Johns Hopkins hospital in Baltimore, Maryland adopted an interesting and effective communications practice within its intensive care unit (ICU). It certainly needed to do something. Patient care was suffering.

Typically, attending physicians would spend 20 to 25 minutes discussing a patient's case with nurses and resident doctors. The discussion covered information about pain control, nutrition, family communication, and care strategies. Shockingly, the care team usually did not fully understand the care plan for the patient—mistakes happened.

A "daily goals form" was devised as a means of overcoming this communications problem. A simple, one-page form outlined a step-by-step daily care plan for each ICU patient. Results improved dramatically.

The hospital conducted a year-long study to measure the effectiveness of this straightforward communications device. It was found that the average length of ICU stay was cut in half and nurse and resident doctor understanding of the daily care plan increased from 10% to over 95%.

Clearly, the form works. It is a great way of helping the care team process a large amount of critical information in a consistent and trouble-free manner. At least 75 other hospitals now use some version of the "daily goals form."

It is exciting to see how organizations such as Johns Hopkins are effectively wrestling with the communication demands of the *Best Practices Era*. What is your enterprise doing to improve communication?

Source: "On the same page," *The Hartford Courant*, Staff and wire reports, p. D3, October 7, 2003.

the organization to leverage its collective knowledge and experiences across generations of employees—promoting a learning environment within the concern.

The trick is to make sure that the lessons learned are documented by every project team doing work in the company and to make sure the chronicle is easily accessible by everyone in the firm. Standardizing the format and location of the *Lessons Learned Chronicle* goes a long way toward institutionalizing the use of this communications vehicle.

Additionally, a lessons learned work step should be made part of every project plan. This helps cement the concept in the "hearts and minds" of any employee who works on a project. In time, the idea spreads and becomes common practice within the organization.

Intranet Bulletin Boards

An electronic bulletin board dealing with various work-related subjects can be established within a firm's intranet and/or e-mail environments. Because many

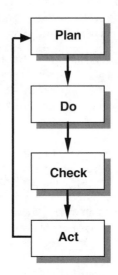

Figure 7.3 A typical quality review process.

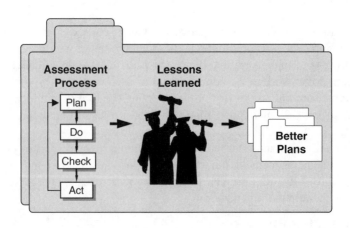

Figure 7.4 The lessons learned should be captured and published.

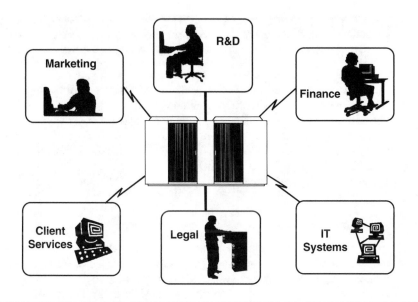

Figure 7.5 The e-bulletin board can be an important broadcast medium.

staff members use the intranet and e-mail on a daily basis, an electronic bulletin board can become a very useful embellishment and a terrific broadcast mechanism.

In fact, many organizations use such devices to solicit improvement ideas from personnel, to transmit newsletters, to distribute results from performance reviews, and to deliver project progress reports to interested constituents (see Figure 7.5).

Executive Information Systems Applications

Executive Information Systems (EIS) applications are automated applications that provide senior executives with the information that they need to run their businesses. EIS applications facilitate the access and integration of a variety of data originating from both inside and outside the company. The systems are constantly monitoring particular facts about the company and automatically inform executives when those facts require their attention.

With a direct line to the upper echelon of an organization, these systems become indispensable communication devices. It is important that a company's communication program deliberately makes use of them and other electronic and wireless systems to improve communications within the enterprise (for recent industry examples, see the Hartford and TELUS sidebars).

BEST PRACTICES BUSINESS IN ACTION

The Hartford: Computerizing Communications

Competition is stiff in the insurance industry, but The Hartford continues to prosper and grow. Its annual revenue is nearly $20 billion dollars and its employee head-count is expected to top 30,000 by the end of 2005.

One of the reasons why the firm has been so successful is that it has been able to effectively spur profitable growth. Ensuring solid company communications is an important element of managing for profit. It is no wonder that the company is constantly searching for ways of improving company communication systems so that everyone in the organization knows what is going on and has an opportunity to contribute ideas and insights.

Here are just few examples of what The Hartford is doing to improve and automate company communications:

- Developed an intranet application to solicit feedback from all its offices on the impact of work process improvements on customers, staff, and product quality
- Built an account management system to provide a mechanism for employees to post and retrieve information on the company's clients and prospects
- Created a database that tracks important information including project status, staff utilization, and lessons learned on all company projects
- Established a competitive intelligence application, complete with financial and news reports, that staff can contribute to and access to gain insights on competitors such as AIG and The Prudential

While it is certain that these systems and databases are not the sole reason for The Hartford's continued success, using these devices as a means of improving communications across the company surely advances the cause. Everyone feels as if they are part of something big. No one is left out.

This kind of *esprit de corps* is an essential underpinning for prosperity of the *Best Practices Enterprise*™. A focus on communications not only improves morale, but also helps instill the discipline that leads to great business achievement—just like that realized by The Hartford.

Road Shows

Another way of informing personnel and other stakeholders about significant business events is to establish an awareness program (or "road show"). A road show will involve the creation of a business briefing that introduces such things as new business initiatives, product launches, and work process changes. The road shows explains the impact these things may have on the business and/or stakeholder community.

Once a road show is planned, it should be presented at convenient locations (both live and virtual) so that all stakeholders interested in attending have easy access (see Figure 7.6). With the right equipment, road shows can be produced

BEST PRACTICES BUSINESS IN ACTION

TELUS Stays Connected

TELUS is Canada's second-largest telecom company. The firm employs over 24,000 staff and manages combined assets of over $10 billion (Canadian). Unsurpassed customer service and outstanding employee job satisfaction are hallmarks of the concern. Unfortunately, service technicians, who spend most of their time in the field, often felt isolated and disconnected from the company. Productivity suffered.

In response, TELUS embarked on an initiative to provide effortless communication capabilities to its field staff. The effort involved providing service technicians with wireless access to the Internet, the intranet, and the automated work administration system, which allows field staff to retrieve work orders and report on job status.

Within its first 4 months of use, the new system allowed TELUS to achieve a 26% increase in repair volume and a 24% increase in appointments met—a clear sign that field staff members were becoming more productive.

As a bonus, service technicians are increasingly more satisfied with their jobs. This is due, in part, to the staff's increased ability to keep abreast of internal company activity through the use of the seamless remote access capabilities of the system.

Certainly, this endeavor will translate into increased customer satisfaction and retention as well. How can one be dissatisfied with a swift response and enhanced efficiency? This *Best Practices Enterprise*™ endeavor demonstrates how results-oriented communications can deliver the goods, when done in a thoughtful and deliberate way.

Source: "Effortless communications—TELUS brings the vision home," *Telecommunications Industry Solutions*, Marketing Brochure, IBM Corporation, 1999.

using the Internet/intranet, video conferencing, and other communications technologies.

Of course, the focus of a road show may be different for different audiences, but the content of the briefing must be consistent. A firm must not mislead or confuse stakeholders when communicating with them. It is just *bad business* to do so.

Newsletters

A newsletter can be created as a means of keeping stakeholders better informed about the business. With this vehicle, news concerning the enterprise can be delivered to the entire stakeholder community in a timely, efficient, and effective way.

But beware! This device is often overused. I have seen firms that produce dozens of departmental newsletters every month. This "waters down" the effectiveness of the communications vehicle. After all, who has time to read three dozen newsletters every month?

Figure 7.6 Road shows take the message to the masses.

It is better to have a single newsletter for the entire firm. It will become the "news authority" for the business. Everyone will read it.

Project Coordination Meetings

Project coordination meetings are another important communications vehicle. As Figure 7.7 suggests, project coordination meetings are held among strategic planners and all company PMs. The purposes of these meetings are to:

- Provide an opportunity for PMs to report any issues that will impact the delivery of their projects.
- Provide strategic planners with an opportunity to coach PMs on how to improve their work.
- Create an environment whereby project managers can meet to discuss cross-project issues and actively identify opportunities for reusing and reapplying parts of their project work in other efforts.

On a quarterly basis, the strategic planners meet with the ESC to share their insights on each of the projects and discuss any necessary adjustments or changes to the firm's projects and strategic plans.

A FEW POINTERS

Now that we have discussed some of the more popular communication devices used by firms today, let us examine a few steps businesses can take to ensure the success of new communication programs:

Executive Steering Committee

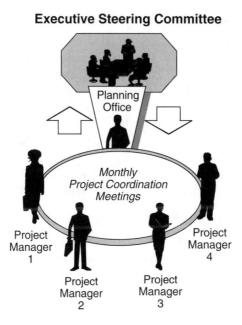

Figure 7.7 The project coordination process.

Convince Staff to Communicate More Often

No one wants to host a party and have no one show up. It can be like that with a new communications program. A firm must promote the new program—convincing the heads of each business area to have their staff put deliberate effort into communicating more often and to make use of the new communications vehicles that have been put into place.

Work to Match the Message with the "Right" Communication Device

Once staff members are used to communicating more often, the challenge will be to match the communication vehicle with the message being sent. Not all communications should be made in the same way. Firms should be careful not to use communication vehicles indiscriminately. Communiqués are more effective when delivered through the most appropriate vehicle available.

For instance, a lay-off notice may be better delivered in person than through a broadcast message pumped out through the company's e-mail system. Similarly, the details about the annual company picnic may be better delivered through the company newsletter than through the senior management's EIS system.

Develop Strategies for Conveying Urgent News

As communications grow, a strategy for delivering important news should be established. The strategy should describe a standard way of conveying information that is of a serious nature. This will help staff discern vital news from that which is provided for informational purposes only—ensuring that critical information gets immediate attention.

Consider the issues surrounding 9/11. In hindsight, it is apparent that the communications infrastructure supporting the "1st Responders" was inadequate. The U.S. government is taking steps to attend to these issues (see the SAFECOM sidebar for additional perspective), but it took a crisis to start the communications strategy work needed improve the situation. Do not wait for a crisis.

Send Serious Information Quickly

Whatever the strategy is for delivering serious news, it should be made available to concerned parties as quickly as possible. Holding back bad news can be deadly to company morale and stakeholder relations. With the emergence of Sarbanes-Oxley regulations and front-page scandals such as those that erupted at Enron, MCI, and Marsh & McLennan, it is in every organization's best interest to communicate early and often.

Create a "Two-Way Street"

True communication happens when the parties involved understand exactly what the other intends. It is a two-way street. Companies must work diligently to establish processes within their communication mechanisms that allow this kind of true "give and take." It is just good communications … and that is good business.

IN CLOSING

A communications program is an important management tool. It establishes the business processes and the communication vehicles necessary for a firm to share and receive information from all its stakeholders in an accurate and effortless way.

As the business world continues to accelerate and interconnect, and the workforce becomes more diverse and independent, it is likely that communication strategies will become crucial to the success of *Best Practices Enterprises*™.

Going forward, we must ensure that our businesses are managing communications deliberately because effective communications strategies may be the difference between success and failure in tomorrow's ultracompetitive marketplace.

* * *

BEST PRACTICES BUSINESS IN ACTION
SAFECOM: U.S. Terrorism Strategy

Overseen by the Department of Homeland Security, SAFECOM is an overarching program within the federal government that oversees all initiatives and projects pertaining to public safety communications and interoperability.

Its mission is to improve public safety response nationwide (across local, tribal, state, and federal organizations) through more effective and efficient interoperable communications.

The events of 9/11 demonstrate that the country faces many challenges in this arena, including:

- Incompatible and aging communications equipment
- Limited and fragmented federal, state, and local budget cycles and funding
- Limited and fragmented federal, state, and local planning and coordination
- Limited and fragmented radio spectrum
- Lack of equipment standards

To address these challenges, the SAFECOM program has developed a Statement of Requirements (SoR) that defines what it will take to achieve full interoperability, initiates communications and interoperability standards, and provides industry requirements against which product vendors can map their product capabilities.

Further, the SAFECOM program has developed the Continuum Guide for Addressing the Interoperability Challenge, which provides a framework for helping local, tribal, state, and federal policy makers address communication issues such as:

- Who needs to talk to whom during an incident?
- Which form (or combination of forms) of media should be used to communicate during a time of crisis?
- Which technologies should be used for communicating and when they should be deployed?

The SAFECOM program is an example of what the federal government is doing to prepare the country for a terrorist attack. Sadly, the threat of terrorism is a *Best Practices Era* challenge as well. But if the federal government can address its communication problems, businesses can too.

Source: Based on information provided on the website www.safecomprgram.gov, February 14, 2005.

This book has free material available from download from the
Web Added Value™ resource center at *www.jrosspub.com*

CROSS-CULTURAL WORKFORCE INCLUSION

*An inclusion effort that addresses the workforce diversity challenge has sprung up as well. It has become a major influence within the company. As a result, **Your Company, Inc**. has been able to develop and retain staff from around the globe, while building sustainable "corporate knowledge" within the firm.*

It is a competitive reality that today's global businesses cross both borders and cultures. The increases in the offshoring of work and the softening of trade barriers are strong indications that the trend will not end any time soon (see India sidebar for a current example). As a result, staff members hail from all sorts of ethnic, educational, and socioeconomic backgrounds, forming a broad and bright mosaic within the *Best Practices Enterprise*™. This medley of skills and talents promotes new ways of thinking and executing. Accordingly, the corporate culture is shifting, evolving, and improving.

Cross-cultural workforce inclusion is the best practice covered in this chapter (see Figure 8.1). It is included because it is important to shed some light on what firms can do to rethink their existing cultural paradigms and recast them in ways that will help organizations benefit from the individual differences that exist among the workforce. The time has come for firms to come to grips with the underlying attitudes, beliefs, and expectations of its personnel and provide the thought leadership needed to ascertain success in the new epoch.

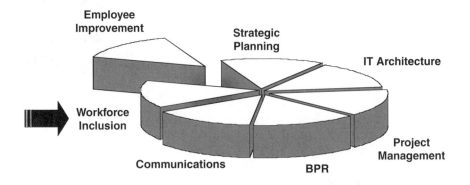

Figure 8.1 Workforce inclusion is another important element.

BEST PRACTICES BUSINESS IN ACTION

India: Call Center to the World

24/7 Customer is a U.S.-based company located in Bangalore, India. It offers customer service outsourcing to its clients around the world. The company is one of hundreds of such operations in India.

An astounding 98% of 24/7's 1300 employees hold college degrees. While India's blossoming customer service/call center industry experiences an 18% annual turnover rate, it still outshines America's 42% turnover for similar work. With an average customer service representative's salary in India at $90 per week, it is difficult to argue the merits of setting up shop there—a highly educated workforce that is willing to work for far less than the going rate elsewhere.

What is more, there is a real interest in neutralizing regional differences in order to improve the customer experience when calling into Indian-based call centers. 24/7, for example, provides on-premises speech classes for its workers. Each staff member goes through weeks of training to even out their native accents and intonations before they ever pick up a phone.

Other call center firms ask Indian employees to adopt American-sounding names (or aliases) during their time on the phone. The thought is that by doing such, customers calling in will feel more at ease and comfortable when discussing the problems that prompted the call in the first place.

This example illustrates just where the global competitive environment is heading. Businesses are doing business everywhere, and from anywhere, through a network of interconnected pieces. Indigenous talent will be leveraged to its fullest, and the customer will be none the wiser. Results are all that matter to a *Best Practices Enterprise*™, regardless of who provides the service or ensures the quality.

Source: Based on "Answering the calls" by Aaron Davis, *San Jose Mercury News, The Hartford Courant*, November 23, 2003, p. D1.

DEFINING THE BUSINESS CASE FOR CROSS-CULTURAL WORKFORCE INCLUSION

First and foremost, cross-cultural workforce inclusion is about leveraging the differences that exist among personnel as a means of gaining a competitive edge in the marketplace. Placing any kind of moral or ethical judgment on the subject only serves to complicate it. Certainly, companies have a social responsibility within the markets they serve. However, the leveraging of a diverse workforce is not an obligation but a choice. Businesses inevitably choose to do whatever is needed to enhance stockholder value. Organizations choose to institute inclusive behavior because it makes for better performing organizations.

With that said, when a concern chooses the pursuit of cross-cultural workforce inclusion, it can expect the following results:

- *Enhanced workforce quality*—The best and brightest are attracted to an attractive work setting. If you become recognized as an employer who develops and promotes a wide array of people, you will have created an attractive work setting and improved workforce quality in the process.
- *Improved performance*—A work environment that fosters inclusion and provides opportunities for staff to be heard and valued will perform better than ones that fail to recognize employees due to differences in age, race, gender, religion, or sexual orientation.
- *Greater access to new markets*—A diverse workforce can introduce a company to a diverse and broad customer base that it may not have reached otherwise. Firms should recruit and retain staff members who reflect the needs and interests of their customers. The diversity of the global marketplace demands that providers understand customer needs and wants.
- *Better decision-making*—Difficult problems and challenges require new and different perspectives. By virtue of greater diversity, a cross-cultural work environment promotes new ways of thinking and doing. New behaviors bring improved decision-making and leadership to an organization.
- *Chic corporate culture*—The differences in thoughts and motivations that come when establishing a workforce comprised of a kaleidoscope of cultures can introduce a level of energy and originality that will make for an irresistible work setting. Such an enterprise is capable of becoming a juggernaut of unsurpassed performance in the marketplace.

Collectively, these elements encompass the business case for implementing cross-cultural workforce inclusion. In the next section, we will look at ways of getting a corporate-wide diversity and inclusion program off the ground.

SETTING THE PROGRAM IN MOTION

How does a global *Best Practices Enterprise*™ establish a culture that best leverages its broadly diverse workforce? An ongoing corporate-wide program is required to make the concepts of cross-cultural workforce inclusion "stick to the wall." The crucial elements of such a program include:

- CEO sponsorship
- Project launch
- Inclusion team
- New behavior paradigm
- Diversity framework strategy
- Program measurement accord
- New culture training and promotion
- Diversity administration

These program components are considered in more detail below.

CEO Sponsorship

Cross-cultural workforce inclusion programs start at the top. Without executive commitment, the corporate culture will not change. Everyone follows the leader. If the CEO adjusts behavior, the stage is set for success.

The executive behaviors most monitored include financial investment in the program, accessibility to project leaders, and visible participation in the change effort. If the senior management team witnesses these behaviors in the CEO they will get behind the effort. If they do not, the change agents promoting the effort are just howling in the woods.

Time must be spent convincing the CEO that diversity and inclusion make sound business sense. Discussing the business case, as discussed above, is the best place to start. Inviting the executive to seminars and using outside experts to assist in the education and awareness effort can also be effective ways of gaining CEO support for the program.

Project Launch

A cross-cultural workforce inclusion program begins with the initial project. The project launch effort must focus on raising staff awareness of the program.

Through directed briefings, employees are educated about the program's business drivers.

They should come to understand that the program will not only improve company performance, but will also enhance their ability to get their job done. Highlighting advancement opportunities and discussing the diminishing of workplace conflicts that the program will bring tend to go a long way in helping staff appreciate the employee benefits of the change effort.

Furthermore, the launch effort should provide a solid definition of diversity and inclusion. The definition of terms helps staff understand what the program is all about. By focusing the discussion on desired behaviors, and less on the "employee differences" element of the program, personnel will adopt a more open attitude toward the program.

Lastly, the project plan should be presented. Knowing tasks and time lines aids staff in understanding what will happen throughout the project duration. They will come to see what is expected of them and recognize the importance of their participation—both keys to ongoing program success.

The Inclusion Team

Once the project is launched, the inclusion team should be formed. It is important for this team to be comprised of a cross-cut of management and staff. The better the team represents all the personnel within a firm, the more likely it is that its recommendations will resonate with the staff.

As the project team for the cross-cultural workforce inclusion program, the inclusion team is responsible for analyzing and synthesizing project findings and developing recommendations for change within the organization. Because the team is capable of sporting great influence within the concern, it is important to consider augmenting it through the use of external diversity consultants. These experts can help in training the team and ensuring the overall quality of the results generated.

As an aside, a team gains instant credibility within an enterprise by attaining the participation of a high-ranking executive as project sponsor. This executive will be responsible for representing senior management's interests in the program and for keeping the communication channels open to the top. The right sponsor can make a difference between program success and failure.

Building a New Behavior Paradigm

The work of establishing a new behavior paradigm, which defines the inclusion-related behavior expectations of the organization, falls squarely on the shoulders of the inclusion team and its executive sponsor. Think of it as a detailed vision statement for diversity and inclusion that outlines expected behavior and desired business results.

Prepared as a multipaged document, the new behavior paradigm should contain principles and value statements about diversity and inclusion. It should contain in-depth scenarios that exemplify interpersonal work interactions and their desired outcomes. The new behavior paradigm should be written to become a referential guide to employee conduct.

The development of a comprehensive and detailed new behavior paradigm is crucial to the long-term success of a cross-cultural workforce inclusion program because much of the subsequent work identified within the program focuses on behavior modification.

Each employee will be required to come to terms with deep-rooted beliefs and attitudes about those who are somehow different or foreign to them. Once staff members come to better understand their own belief systems, they will be directed to begin to recognize the behaviors that their belief system supports and fosters. With new perspectives in hand, personnel can work to adjust their own behavior to better align with that which is defined in the new behavior paradigm.

Crafting the Diversity Framework Strategy

Crafting the diversity framework strategy document is the next order of business for the inclusion team. A diversity framework strategy contains three elements: a current workplace assessment, needs analysis, and recommendations for action. This document is the "nuts and bolts" of the cross-cultural workforce inclusion program. It provides a road map for what is to follow from the program.

The current workplace assessment effort gathers data from the organization's existing diversity and inclusion activities. Often done in cross-departmental workshops and through employee surveys, the assessment element of the diversity framework strategy provides rich commentary on the current state of affairs within the *Best Practices Enterprise™*. It provides the fodder for the recommendations that need to be established.

The needs analysis work is characterized by the benchmarking of the firm's existing practices against those of competitors and key customers in the marketplace. The goal is to gain an understanding of the practices, tools, and measurement systems that are available and being used within similar organizations. By benchmarking, an enterprise can establish what it may need within its cross-cultural workforce inclusion program in order to remain competitive.

The recommendations for action element of the diversity framework strategy contain the plan of suggested activities that the organization should perform in order to establish the cultural change that it seeks. Typically, recommendations include such work as training initiatives, adjustments to hiring/retention/promotion procedures, and mentoring programs. Nonetheless, all the recommendations for action must be anchored in the reality that the business is required to continue to exceed customer expectations while recasting its corporate culture.

Program Measurement Accord

The development of a program measurement accord is critical to the continued success of the cross-cultural workforce inclusion program. Created by the inclusion team, a *program measurement accord* document defines measurable objectives for each initiative defined in the diversity framework strategy, describes how the measurement criteria will be collected, and discusses how measurement results will be utilized to adjust subsequent diversity initiatives.

The objectives defined for each initiative should be concrete and quantifiable. Some examples include:

- Increasing employee satisfaction by 20% through the introduction of an incivility awareness program
- Reducing minority turnover by 15% through a minorities-focused retention program
- Escalating top line growth by 10% via the augmentation of the sales associate education program with a new diversity training module

With the objectives defined, it is important to make clear the means of collecting measurement data. Satisfaction surveys, focus groups, and the simple quantification of statistics and financials are legitimate ways of collecting and amalgamating the measurements.

Each measurement review should be used to provide input that will shape future diversity initiatives. By folding an evaluation process into every cross-cultural workforce inclusion program project, a global organization becomes better positioned to make diversity and inclusion an integral and enduring part of the corporate culture.

Clearly, the ongoing evaluation of a cross-cultural workforce inclusion program will characteristically be demanding. However, it is compulsory to maintain the momentum needed to renovate a corporate culture that is naturally resistant to change.

New Culture Training and Promotion

Diversity training and the formal promotion of the cross-cultural workforce inclusion program are important success factors of all inclusion efforts. After all, a new corporate culture is being forged through such programs, and it will require support and nurturing in order to take root.

The training efforts recommended in the diversity framework strategy document should be two-pronged. Some training dollars should be allocated to raising the staff's awareness and understanding of workplace diversity, while other training investments should be aimed at skills development and behavior modification.

By addressing training topics such as diffusing workplace animosity, improving active listening skills, and a manager's guide to promoting from within, an

BEST PRACTICES BUSINESS IN ACTION
Up Close and Personal at Kraft Foods

The Northfield, Illinois-based Kraft Foods is best known for its Maxwell House Coffee, Keebler Cookies, and Kraft Macaroni & Cheese Dinner brands. It is also becoming recognized for developing talent from within. Its latest initiative targets the development of women and people of color.

Using a technique that it calls "Up Close and Personal" sessions, Kraft gathers small groups of employees together with an executive of similar ethnic and racial backgrounds. The sessions allow the employees to engage in meaningful dialogue with senior managers about the issues and challenges that must be faced and overcome in order to get ahead in business.

Interestingly, each 90-minute session is recorded and any tidbits of advice or lessons learned that come out of the sessions are then shared with the rest of the organization through the employee intranet and the company's various diversity councils. In this way, Kraft intends to keep its diversity mentoring efforts current and vital.

The Up Close and Personal sessions are already paying dividends. These sessions have led to the creation of myriad diversity, staff development, personnel recruitment, and retention strategies. The company's efforts are a clear indication that multinational organizations must embrace diversity and inclusion as a means of remaining competitive in the *Best Practices Business Era*. To put it simply, "It is just good business!"

Source: Based on "Getting 'up close and personal' develops talent: Janice Fenn," by C. Stone Brown, Diversity Inc., May 2005, p. 98.

organization focuses its efforts on improving behaviors that enhance productivity and the overall work environment.

While training can be provided in finite parts over an extended period of time, the work of promoting the cross-cultural workforce inclusion program is never finished. Many organizations establish task forces, special interest worker groups, and diversity councils and sponsor fireside chats as means of keeping the internal public relations fires burning. Three recent examples from industry are presented in the sidebars.

Regardless of the training and promotion approaches taken, the worker population should be provided with ample opportunity to better understand diversity and inclusion issues and improve their skills foundation (a few of these points are further developed in the real-world examples provided in the Kraft Foods, Ford, and BP examples).

BEST PRACTICES BUSINESS IN ACTION

Employee Resource Groups at Ford Motor Company

Ford Motor Company is gaining some mileage from its employee resource groups (ERGs). The ERGs are comprised of Ford employees and can be thought of as special interest groups that are intended to help the company better meet the needs and expectations of its diverse workforce.

Ford's current ERGs include:

- Ford-Employees African American Network (FAAN)
- Hispanic Network Group (HNG)
- Ford Asian Indian Association (FAIA)
- Ford Chinese Association (FCA)
- Ford Gay, Lesbian or Bi-Sexual Employees (GLOBE)
- Ford Parenting Network (FPN)
- Professional's Women's Network (PWN)
- Ford Interfaith Network (FIN)

These groups are being supported by the firm's Executive Council on Diversity and Work Life (ECD). Recognizing the value that such groups can have in promoting diversity initiatives within the firm, the ECD provides financial aid and an executive champion for every group.

Ford's ECD hopes that these groups can help the company recruit and retain the best talent available in the marketplace and that through special projects the ERGs will contribute to the betterment of the organization.

The company's investments in the ERGs are already providing a return. Recently, the FCA group provided assistance and translation services to executives who were meeting with Chinese dignitaries, and the GLOBE group provided insight into the development of the firm's same-sex healthcare benefits public announcements to be disseminated throughout the company.

Unquestionably, the Ford example is just one of many that support the notion that diversity and inclusion is a competitive imperative in the global marketplace of the *Best Practices Enterprise*™.

Source: Based on "Employee resource groups are finding support in ECD," www.fordglobe.org, 2001.

Diversity Administration

Once the cross-cultural workforce inclusion program is up and running and the work of the Inclusion Team is complete, the responsibility for maintaining and extending the program must be established. There is some debate over just where that responsibility should lie.

Predictably, the human resource department is the easy answer. But choosing HR to oversee ongoing diversity and inclusion efforts has its limitations. Sometimes staff members do not have much faith in the skills and competence

BEST PRACTICES BUSINESS IN ACTION
The "Race Summit" at BP

British Petroleum (BP) is involved in the exploration and production of crude oil and natural gas and in the manufacturing and marketing of petrochemicals. It is also very committed to its diversity and inclusion initiatives. BP wants to be the employer, partner, and supplier of choice in all the countries where it operates.

An early adopter of inclusion programs, BP understands the value of establishing a diverse workforce and leveraging it to its full potential in order to continue to achieve outstanding results. As a global concern, BP recognizes that it is competing for the best talent available throughout the world, and it has taken broad steps to deliberately make diversity and inclusion a natural element of its work environment.

In 2003 and 2004, for example, the firm held a series of what it called "race summits" across the United States. The meetings involved staff and management from around the company. Discussions focused on addressing issues of race and driving a healthy dialogue on the subject. Postsummit surveys showed that nearly 98% of attendees found the meetings to be positive and a truly unique experience. It is estimated that over 10,000 BP staff members have participated in discussions about race as a direct consequence of these summits.

Clearly, the race summits represent a solid step forward for the company. There is still much to do at BP to keep its workforce primed for the challenges of the global market environment. But, in the words of Emily Deakin, BP's General Manager of Diversity & Inclusion, and a prime mover behind the summits, "... it's not about building a color-blind BP. It's about acknowledging and benefiting from the differences...." Indeed, that is what diversity and inclusion is all about.

Source: Based on "Emily Deakin, General Manager Diversity & Inclusion, reflects on the 'race issue' in the US," www.bp.com, 2005.

of the department. Moreover, the move to place responsibility with the HR department may serve to further confuse employees who see diversity work as nothing more than another version of affirmative action. Regardless of the reason, program credibility can suffer when diversity administration is left in the hands of the HR department.

If at all possible, placing diversity administration responsibility in the lap of the CEO is a better choice. This is not to suggest that the CEO should assume the responsibility directly, although that could be done. Rather, the CEO should be responsible for determining who among his staff will be made responsible for diversity administration.

In this way, staff will come to see visible support and interest among the senior management team, which helps establish instant credibility for the program. Furthermore, with senior management enrolled, organizational obstacles are directly cleared, core competences are more easily developed, and continuing funding needs are better met.

In the next section, we will explore more specific ways this idea can be leveraged to maintain the momentum of corporate-wide diversity and inclusion efforts.

MAINTAINING MOMENTUM THROUGH CORPORATE OFFICER DESIGNATION

How does an organization maintain the momentum established by a well-orchestrated cross-cultural workforce inclusion program? Diversity work is best fortified by creating the institutional elements that will keep the spirit of the program in the forefront of thought and action within the concern. What better way of putting the necessary elements in place than by designating a new officer title and implementing the associated apparatus that supports the position?

Chief Diversity Officer

The chief diversity officer (CDO) reports to the CEO and is responsible for overseeing the cross-cultural workforce inclusion program and all its projects and programs. The position should have some teeth and influence within the organization. It cannot be a position that is reduced to having only committee sponsorship responsibility.

Becoming involved in strategic initiatives that are not specifically diversity-related is one way of being sure that the CDO position gets its due. In this way, the position gains visibility and reach. Diversity and inclusion issues underpin most work, and through participation and representation, the CDO has a direct opportunity to be heard and to provide perspective.

A second way of bolstering the influence of the position is for the CDO to stay on top of the measurement elements of the cross-cultural workforce inclusion program. A CDO can gain the respect of his of her peers by becoming an authority on the program and what it is doing for the organization. Having the measurement information readily available also goes a long way in gaining the investment commitment for ongoing diversity and inclusion work.

Office of Diversity and Inclusion

The Office of Diversity and Inclusion (ODI) reports to the CDO. It is responsible for cross-cultural workforce inclusion program administration. ODI staff members are the diversity and inclusion "experts" within an enterprise. The office is most effective when it possesses core knowledge of the issues and has the skills to drive the cultural transformation effort.

Because individuals possessing such knowledge and skills are often difficult to find, many ODIs employ consultants to provide the necessary coaching. By employing a *player/coach model*, one where consultants work alongside internal personnel, global organizations gain the benefits of a consultant's work, while developing their own expertise.

Diversity and Inclusion Charter

Under the direction of the CDO, the ODI is also responsible for crafting the organization's diversity and inclusion charter. The charter, a one-page corporate document, is fashioned after a standard mission statement. It outlines a firm's commitment to diversity and inclusion. It should also state that the organization values its entire workforce and is committed to creating a workplace that leverages all the skills and talents of its people so as to maximize competitive gain.

Tying diversity and inclusion to the competitive gain of the enterprise is imperative. It sets a tone that such work is about making the company better and improving its performance. It helps personnel understand that besides being the right thing to do, diversity and inclusion is a vital element of the competitive landscape.

The diversity and inclusion charter is important not because of its "motherhood and apple pie" appeal, but also because it symbolically puts a stake in the ground. It marks an organization as one that is committed to diversity and inclusion. It will serve to attract like-minded individuals to the *Best Practices Enterprise™*—potential employees and prospective clients alike.

Diversity-in-Action Recognition Programs

Program promotion is an essential part of the CDO position. The creation of a diversity-in-action recognition program, which acknowledges achievements in diversity and inclusion efforts within the company, is a fine way of advancing such work.

Recognition can be bestowed on individuals, work teams, or entire departments. By making awards very public, the organization is declaring that diversity and inclusion work is valued. Public recognition serves to reinforce new behaviors in other staff members and rewards early adopters for their effort.

What is actually given as an award is less important than the recognition that comes with earning it. Many organizations give reward plaques or some other small token that can be displayed in one's office. Other businesses couple that with cash, gift certificates, or tickets to sporting or entertainment events. Regardless, it is the recognition that matters. Promotion is needed to overcome resistance and roadblocks.

WATCH FOR ROADBLOCKS

Because people are ethnocentric (i.e., we judge the world through what is familiar to us), the work of building an inclusive corporate culture is extremely difficult. Couple this with the fact that we are all naturally resistant to change, and one begins to truly understand the challenges that cross-cultural workforce inclusion programs regularly face. All kinds of organizational obstructions are created in an effort to stall and resist such programs.

Often taking many forms, the most common roadblocks for cross-cultural workforce inclusion programs include:

- Ineffective executive support
- Process deficiencies
- Worker burnout
- Insufficient training
- Misunderstanding the EEOC (Equal Employment Opportunity Commission)

Let us look at each of these to gain perspective.

Ineffective Executive Support

The CDO position must be staffed by a charismatic and involved senior manager who approaches the job with sincerity and vigor. The CDO must work to gain the respect of peers and subordinates alike. In the end, this person is the "chief cheerleader" of the entire cross-cultural workforce inclusion program. If there is only lukewarm enthusiasm at the top, how can an organization expect to change its culture for the better?

Process Deficiencies

Cross-cultural workforce inclusion programs only work within the proper context. Fundamental HR-related processes including job posting/internal promotion procedures, corporate training, and mentoring programs must be in place and fully functional for a diversity program to take hold. Inclusion programs rely on these fundamentals and will use them as a means of providing a framework for diversity initiatives.

Worker Burnout

Employee stress and worker burnout can stand in the way of cross-cultural workforce inclusion program success. Outsourcing, merger, and downsizing efforts all contribute to personnel stress. In fact, even rumors that such an event is in the works are devastatingly distractive. So, choose the timing of program launch soundly and watch for worker burnout. Staff will not respond well if they are pulled in too many directions.

Insufficient Training

Diversity and inclusion training must be aimed at the entire employee population. Every worker must come to understand the broad issues of the program and its importance to the business and be given the opportunity to develop the necessary skills for modifying behavior in accordance with enterprise needs. If the training fails to provide these to personnel, all kinds of unexpected problems may arise (see the Diversity and Inclusion sidebar for a recent example). It is essential that training be well designed and executed early in the cross-cultural workforce inclusion program.

Misunderstanding EEOC

The EEOC was established by the federal government to oversee affirmative action in the workplace and ensure that work discrimination is completely eliminated in the U.S. Unfortunately, some people may mistake a cross-cultural workforce inclusion program for EEOC and affirmative action efforts.

Indeed, some may boycott the program, choosing not to become involved, because they believe the company is only going through the motions to satisfy a governmental requirement. Here again, training and awareness must be appropriately aimed at helping personnel overcome such misplaced opposition.

In the end, the diversity game can be won. However, it takes hard work and perseverance.

WINNING THE DIVERSITY GAME

The diversity and inclusion game is won when an organization establishes a diverse and inclusive corporate culture. This requires that the organization be comprised of diverse and inclusive people. A diverse workforce can be created by default. After all, the global marketplace demands diversity. However, a diverse workforce developed through deliberate effort will likely be a more powerful force to be reckoned with in the marketplace.

There are multitudes of ways of orchestrating the development and retention of a broadly diverse workforce. Some successful ideas that many organizations are employing include:

- Re-examining job postings and descriptions (adjusting them as needed) to ensure that they truly reflect the skills and talents needed by the organization and that they do not somehow limit competent people from applying

BEST PRACTICES BUSINESS IN ACTION

When Diversity and Inclusion Become Adversity and Delusion

I have been watching a client battle to retool its corporate culture. One of its current initiatives includes a diversity and inclusion program that is aimed at helping the firm form a high-performance work setting that capitalizes on the diversity of the individuals constituting its workforce.

The program, still in its early stages, has pointed to a need for establishing a culture where individual differences among workers are recognized as valuable ingredients in achieving the best business outcomes for the company.

This is, of course, a dramatic departure from the position most companies are in today in regard to managing workforce diversity. It seems that most of the organizations that I have had an opportunity to work with have adopted a "color blindness" and "gender neutrality" that seems to have the effect of ignoring rather than recognizing and leveraging individual employee differences. When the goals of this program are truly realized, the company that I am speaking about will surely have an edge over its competition.

But beware! These kinds of strategic initiatives, like any significant cultural change, are susceptible to misinterpretation. Because momentous change does not happen overnight, many good-intentioned people can get in the way of true transformation.

The diversity and inclusion program can quickly become the "adversity and delusion" program if the organization does not remain diligent in evolving itself through the stages of maturity that such change management requires and allow the thoughts and principles that underpin the initiative to become better understood and communicated across the concern.

Because of its inherent nuances, it is likely that many individuals will interpret the diversity and inclusion program to be about the democratization of consensus building—an environment where every worker has an equal "vote" in decision-making and direction setting. Nothing, of course, could be further from the truth!

In fact, diversity and inclusion is really about disagreement. It is promoting the notion that it is acceptable to disagree (diversity) as long as everyone has an opportunity to contribute their ideas and thoughts and that those contributions are recognized and considered equally, regardless of the contributor (inclusion).

Obviously, some workers may falsely think that they will now have a "say" in direction setting, and those workers possessing more experience and knowledge (and who, indeed, have decision-making responsibility) may face extreme adversity as they attempt to continue to set the right direction. They can be called to task for not being inclusive by those who are feeling excluded (under a misinformed definition of inclusion).

- Making certain that all promotional materials visually reflect diversity and inclusion
- Using diversity-related success stories in company PR campaigns
- Sponsoring and participating in ethnic studies programs at local colleges
- Placing college interns and co-op students who represent diverse groups
- Establishing associations with government programs that train and develop diverse groups
- Designing and promoting employee referral processes that will serve to introduce prospective employees to the firm
- Ensuring that the organization provides diversity training, establishes a diversity charter, and rewards diversity efforts within the enterprise

Regardless of the techniques used, it is important that businesses establish reputations for being diversely populated and inclusive. With such a reputation, it is much easier to attract and retain the talent that is needed. Qualified and capable people seek out such organizations. They want to take part in the fun and excitement.

IN CLOSING

It is clear that the emerging global economy will bring a broad level of employee diversity to the workplace. *Best Practices Enterprise*™ programs such as cross-cultural workforce inclusion assist organizations in rethinking existing cultural paradigms, reconstituting corporate cultures in ways that enable business leaders to take advantage of new and improved personnel attitudes and work practices.

Keep in mind that a corporate culture that ignores emerging diversity and inclusion issues will likely distress earnings and blight the bottom line. An enterprise cannot remain competitive on a global scale by sticking its head in the sand when it comes to this issue. Personnel investment is far too great to overlook the full and proper leveraging of every employee regardless of race, creed, gender, age, or sexual orientation.

The focus on personnel-related best practices continues in the next chapter with an examination of continuous employee improvement.

* * *

CONTINUOUS EMPLOYEE IMPROVEMENT

A continuous employee improvement program has been established. It centers on behavior modification through training and performance measurement, in an environment where business results become the only focus, not some sort of unintended by-product of the work performed.

Continuous employee improvement (CEI) is the seventh business fundamental of focus within the *Best Practices Enterprise*™ philosophy. As Figure 9.1 suggests, it is the last piece of the pie. It is about staff development and measurement. In a nutshell, a well-structured CEI program prepares employees to deliver expected results, tracks performance against those expected results, and rewards personnel when outstanding results are delivered.

Current corporate training and performance measurement paradigms seldom work that way. Most are not integrated; they place emphasis only on training and measuring on a work step basis. At best, these types of approaches offer only incremental improvement opportunities. In fact, it seems that many programs have lost sight of the overall business results being sought by the organizations that have implemented them.

CEI, on the other hand, brings together training and work measurement activities, integrating them into a mutually dependent whole aimed at changing behaviors and improving business performance (see Eskom sidebar for a real-world example).

Let us explore how CEI programs work.

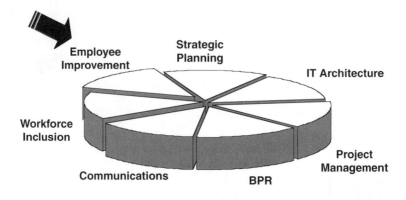

Figure 9.1 The employee improvement program completes the picture.

BEST PRACTICES BUSINESS IN ACTION

Eskom Transforms through Investments in Human Capital

South Africa's electrical utility, Eskom, is in a period of transition-shifting from central government control to a more open, competitive environment. With a new-found emphasis on performance, the utility is focusing effort on retooling its personnel to more effectively compete on an international stage.

Eskom chose to launch a human capital study as a means of beginning its transformation. The study included an examination of the costs associated with human resource development and included an analysis of workforce effectiveness and alignment with corporate strategy. The study concluded with a set of recommendations for improving workers' capabilities and overall work performance.

The resultant human capital strategy strongly called out the need to develop general business, engineering, and project management skills within the workplace. It identified the HR department as the responsible area for overseeing employee development and driving the change effort for the organization.

Up for the task and excited about the possibilities, Eskom is a fine example of CEI in action. By developing key skills and enhancing leadership capabilities the organization is preparing for its entry into the *Best Practices Era's* global marketplace.

Source: Based on "Eskom: Identifying human capital investments that will drive performance," www.accenture.com, 2004.

THE CONTINUOUS EMPLOYEE IMPROVEMENT CONTINUUM

CEI is best presented as a continuum. As Figure 9.2 suggests, CEI is organized into five continuously performed and monitored work steps:

- *Planning step*—It is here that the implementation of the CEI program is devised. Because a CEI program is executed on an ongoing basis, the CEI implementation plan can be put into action in phases. The initial phases of the program tend to focus on the identification of basic training and education needs as determined by the firm's stated strategic direction. Appropriate performance measurements are determined next. These need to be tied to the target business results sought by the enterprise. Later phases of the CEI program will be aimed at refining the training, the performance measurement criteria, and the data collection methods.
- *Execution step*—This step is aimed at the roll-out and implementation of the CEI plan. In early iterations of the continuum, effort will be focused on raising staff awareness and setting a foundation for proper training and measurement. Later, the emphasis will switch to driving the implementation of more sophisticated training and performance measurement initiatives.
- *Measurement step*—The effectiveness of the training and performance measurement activities are evaluated in this step. It is intended to ensure that the two activities are integrated properly and that

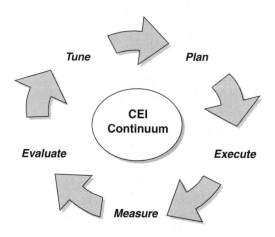

Figure 9.2 The CEI continuum.

> ### BEST PRACTICES BUSINESS IN ACTION
> #### Continuous Employee Improvement at Audi AG
>
> Since its inception in Germany in 1909, Audi AG has been recognized around the world as a high-end, premium-brand automobile manufacturer. This kind of reputation is not gained by accident. The automaker has continued to remain diligent in developing its human resource capabilities over the years.
>
> Recently, the firm has put in place a sophisticated CEI program. The program includes recruitment, selection, training, and job promotion elements. Audi wants to ensure that it is well positioned to continue to deliver exceptional products and services to its highly discerning customer base.
>
> Apprenticeships are the centerpiece of the recruitment and selection components of the automaker's CEI program. Focused on key business functions, the apprenticeships provide Audi with both a "try before you buy" opportunity in recruitment and selection, while affording the automaker the prospect of developing young talent the Audi way.
>
> The training process begins with a supervisor survey that identifies skills deficits and training needs. Appropriate training and coaching is provided to personnel based on the outcome of the surveys. Once trained, staff members are given objectives that will be used to monitor performance and measure improvement.
>
> The job promotion part of the CEI program makes use of formal career paths to define the job promotion conduits for its staff. The technique allows employees to progress through the company in a fair and consistent way while they mature and grow.
>
> Clearly, Audi AG is an organization on the move. It continues to strive by developing the skills and talents needed for success in the new millennium. By embracing best practices concepts, the automaker is sure to be around for the long haul and its staff will prepared for the future.
>
> **Source:** Based on "Audi: Investment in people and in brands," *The Times 100* Edition 8, www.tt100.biz, 2004.

desired business results are being delivered. Any differences between expected and actual results are noted as are any causal relationships that may be observed.

- *Evaluation step*—The outcome of the measurement step is fed into this step for assessment. Potential opportunities for improvement and enhancement are identified and put into priority order based on significance, interdependences among potential improvements, and implementation cost and ease.
- *Tuning step*—With the completion of the evaluation step, appropriate adjustments in training and/or performance measurement initiatives are determined and respective execution plans are tuned accordingly. With the needed alterations in place, the CEI process is repeated.

The CEI continuum continues to iterate in this fashion, evolving with ever more sophistication through each cycle. In time, result-oriented training and performance evaluation is woven into the core of an enterprise's culture (see Audi sidebar for an example). It is at that point that the CEI process shifts from something done deliberately to something that is just simply done—it becomes the way "it" works.

In the next section, we will explore the key planning elements that go into devising a solid CEI strategy.

CEI STRATEGY PLANNING

How does a *Best Practices Enterprise*™ make CEI an essential cultural fundamental? Success is made or broken in the planning of the CEI strategy. An initial CEI strategy is established in the planning step of the first iteration of the CEI continuum. It is refined, over time, as the continuum reiterates.

The basic work steps in developing an initial CEI strategy include:

- Baseline evaluation
- Skills assessment
- CEI program development

Each of these work steps is considered in more detail below.

Baseline Evaluation

When setting CEI into motion, it is important that a snapshot be taken of the entire current work environment. In this way, an organization can evaluate the nature of its starting point and begin to better understand the types of training required and the potential integration points between its measurement and training activities.

A baseline evaluation includes an honest surveying of the existing work setting, both internal and external, and a frank assessment of the current situation. Each facet is appraised based on intent, effectiveness, perceived value, and relationship to strategic direction of the enterprise. Those activities deemed to be most effective and valuable are designated for continuation (where it can be folded into the CEI program), and those that are less effective and do not tie well with the strategic direction are marked for retirement.

The baseline evaluation process helps inform the direction that needs to be taken within the CEI program (see Appendix D for an example of a baseline assessment document).

Skills Assessment

Skills assessment work is another course of action that helps inform the direction of the CEI program. It should be done in conjunction with, or just following, the baseline evaluation. Its focus is to evaluate the adequacy of personnel skill sets and determine any deficiencies that may exist there.

Existing performance evaluations are reviewed and overall operational efficiency is examined and compared with the expected business results as discerned from current business plans and strategic objectives. Any shortcomings are noted, and suggested areas of focus are identified.

With a baseline and skills assessment established, an organization can begin to identify the individual program elements that will be implemented within its CEI program.

Continuous Employee Improvement Program Development

The programs identified for inclusion within a CEI program will differ among organizations. However, all CEI programs will include these elements:

- Competitive analysis
- Performance measurement practices
- Reward and incentive practices
- Recruitment practices
- Retention practices
- Training practices

Let us explore each of these elements.

Competitive analysis

The competitive analysis element of the CEI program determines where other organizations stand in regard to employee performance evaluation, reward/compensation, and training practices.

CEI-focused competitive analysis is done periodically—every year or two is sufficient to keep abreast of the latest trends and innovations in measurement, reward, and training. Information is gathered in both formal and informal ways, including:

- *A recruitment advertisement review* provides basic information about what other organizations are doing.
- *New hire surveys* help gather insight from staff members who have worked for other firms.
- The *professional networking* that takes place through user group participation and seminar attendance gives another perspective on the competition's practices.

- The use of *outside consulting firms* who specialize in such matters offers an objective viewpoint that is invaluable.

Once gathered, competitive analysis findings are organized into two parts: the first part provides insight into the practices of direct competitors and other industry participant firms; and the second part presents results from all other organizations that compete for talent within the regional area. With this information, an enterprise better understands what the measurement, reward, and training standards are within its industry and local marketplace and can use this insight to better fashion its own practices.

Performance measurement practices

The performance measurement practices that are put into place through the CEI program must be tied to desired business outcomes. This implies that standard business objectives such as enhanced profitability, reduced cost-of-operations, improved service and product quality, increased productivity, and faster response/cycle time must be factored into the measurement criteria to be implemented. Similarly, the measures used must provide meaningful insight into staff performance, be validated by data, be cost-effective to capture, and be deemed acceptable by the management team. With that said, time must be taken to thoughtfully and creatively design performance measurement procedures that are appropriate and effective.

An effective performance measurement procedure documents what is being measured (measurement criteria), why it is being measured (objective), and how the measurement data will be captured (measurement mechanism). It also provides the metric to be used and the setting in which the measurement derives its meaning.

Figure 9.3 provides three different measurement procedure examples. These examples are derived from actual organizations. Each is very different in style. Each represents just one of many measurements used to evaluate personnel within its setting.

Measurement procedures typically differ in style and operate not exclusively, but within a network of other procedures. This is done by design in order to provide the most comprehensive picture of staff performance.

Because CEI is an ongoing process, the results of each performance measurement procedure must be monitored, evaluated, and enhanced for improvement on a continual basis. Provisions must be built into every procedure to accommodate this need.

Reward and incentive practices

Rewards and incentives are the other side of the performance measurement. They are the "carrot at the end of the stick." Taking many forms, from a "pat on the

What	Objective	Metric	How	Setting
Measure worker efficiency by *average production cycle time*	Time-to-Market Improvement	Cycle time/number of widgets	Capture process start times, end times, and number of widgets produced	Manufacturer s Shop Floor
Measure worker effectiveness by *average cost per case*	Expense Reduction Improvement	(Total settlement payout + outside fees + actual labor cost)/number of closed cases	Capture payout, outside fees, and labor cost by employee	Insurance Company s Claims Processing Office
Measure staff effectiveness by *average calls received per month following new form introduction*	Service Improvement	(Total phone calls received/ average phone calls received per month) — 1	Capture monthly totals; compare to an average to determine differences	State Tax Department s Forms Development Unit

Figure 9.3 Sample performance measurement procedures.

back" to financial imbursement, rewards and incentives fuel the fire of outstanding performance. People crave recognition and praise. It validates what they do and who they are. Providing acknowledgment in a deliberate way, through the crafting of a well-defined reward and incentive system, is a powerful motivation tool that should be added to every organization's CEI program strategy.

Careful consideration must be applied in designing reward and incentive practices. They must have a strong context in order to be effective. Indeed, rewards and incentives must be strongly tied to organizational strategy and reinforce the behaviors that the management team most desires in its personnel. As Pavlov's experiments proved, behaviors that are consistently rewarded will be repeated.

There are many ways of rewarding and recognizing performance. Notes, plaques, and honorable mentions in company newsletters are a means of publicly recognizing performance. In some organizations that is all that is necessary to inspire staff. Other *Best Practices Enterprises*™ may need to establish more extensive incentive, including cash bonuses, spa days, gift certificates, and additional paid leave. Regardless of the rewards bestowed, tangible, sincere, and consistent recognition for a job well done will serve to reinforce management expectations and will ultimately improve business results.

The value of fairness and consistency in the rewards and incentives system cannot be overestimated. If staff see the recognition practices as being equitably administered, then healthy competition will arise among staff and work groups—morale and performance will improve. If staff thinks that the practices are unfair or encourage favoritism, then morale and productivity will decline. One should not lose sight of this when incorporating reward and incentive practices into a firm's CEI program.

Recruitment practices

Often overlooked, recruitment practices are another essential element of CEI programs. Once a management team has a business strategy and knows where it is heading, it can determine the types of individuals that it needs for success. Some of the individuals needed are among existing employees; some will need to be hired. For this reason it is important to tightly weave the recruitment process into CEI programs.

Besides yielding better results, a recruiting process that is fully integrated into a CEI program becomes a management tool that can be used to directly affect the culture of the organization. It provides a means of attracting and hiring staff in a more purposeful and calculated way—allowing for shaping and molding the workforce as needed.

There are countless ways in which firms recruit talent, including:

- Classified print ads
- Internet job search services
- Home web page job postings
- Open houses
- Public relations/general media
- Job fairs
- Job hotlines
- Customer referrals
- Employee referrals
- Trade school/college relations

Regardless of the technique(s) employed, it is essential that the recruiting effort be specific and directed (as informed by the concern's business strategy). In this way, an organization will attract personnel that meet the needs and fit well within the corporate culture.

Retention practices

Like recruitment processes, retention practices are an important piece of the CEI puzzle that is often lost or forgotten. It seems that CEIs that focus on training and measurement can lead some organizations to leave other facets of staff development out of the picture when designing program content.

It is indisputable that unanticipated staff departures wreak havoc on an organization. Work disruptions, diminished quality, and knowledge losses are just the tip of the iceberg. The effect that key personnel turnover has on employee morale and business preservation can be devastating. For these reasons, retention practices must be carefully developed and incorporated into a firm's CEI program.

The most effective retention efforts direct attention toward:

- Varied and challenging work assignments
- Employee recognition
- Fairness of rules and operating procedures
- Senior management access
- Empowerment/decision-making independence
- Skills/career development
- Articulation of visionary strategic plan and direction
- Work–family policies

The specific retention practices put into place by an organization are situational. Work setting, business location, and the nature of the work itself all have an effect on the type of retention practices required. Some organizations require more sophisticated techniques such as stock option compensation models, job rotation programs, and in-house child day care; others get by with simpler approaches including flextime, casual dress code, and tuition reimbursement. Nevertheless, the design of an explicit retention process is a vital element of CEI strategy, and it should not be left to chance.

Training practices

Clearly, training is a critical facet of all CEI programs. Organizations must be in the business of continually improving their workforces' talents and capabilities. It is the only way that management teams can ensure that their enterprises possess the human capital needed to exceed customer expectations and meet shifting market demands.

Corporate training processes encompass a wide range of practices. The more popular practices include:

- In-house training/seminars
- On-the-job training
- e-Learning

- College/continuing education
- Industry seminars/conferences
- Employee mentoring
- Consultant-guided coaching
- Self-study

Regardless of the practice employed, it is important that training and education be aimed at developing both currently required skills and those that will be essential to the enterprise in the future. The best training and education practices are those that are on-demand, self-paced, and are provided just-in-time. Learning endures when training and education are readily applied (see DaimlerChrysler sidebar for more).

Once all of the specific implementation initiatives that fall out of these six fundamental CEI Program development elements are identified—competitive analysis, performance measurement practices, reward and incentive practices, recruitment practices, retention practices, and training practices—they are put

BEST PRACTICES BUSINESS IN ACTION

Training On-Demand at DaimlerChrysler

Automobile manufacturer DaimlerChrysler is located in Auburn Hills, Michigan. It uses PeopleSoft's Payroll and Human Capital Management software in support and administration of its 96,000 employees. Training new staff on the use of these tools has always been problematic because the automaker's offices are located throughout the world.

In response, the firm has developed a virtual, web-based training curriculum to meet the need. Today, DaimlerChrysler staff can gain system training on demand via the Internet. Additionally, the educational materials available on the web have proven to be a fine source of first-cut systems documentation for the user community as well.

The business benefits of this training program have been immediately felt. They include:

- Easement of timing restrictions through on-demand training capability
- Improved training results through self-paced training management
- Elimination of geographic limitations through location-independent training delivery
- Overall cost savings through the better use of technology

DaimlerChrysler's web-based training solution serves as an example of the creative things that businesses are doing in the realm of CEI. By investing in its employee's education and development, the manufacturer is investing in its future— a *Best Practices Business* imperative.

Source: Based on "Profile: DaimlerChrysler," www.peoplesoft.com, 2004.

into priority order and placed on a time line for execution. As each initiative commences, it is continually monitored and improved upon through iterations of the CEI continuum.

In the next section, we will explore how CEI programs are best launched and administered as well as the cultural implications that these programs have on organizations that embrace the concepts underpinning CEI.

DRIVING THE CEI PROGRAM

Within most organizations, the CEI program is driven from the human resource department. There is nothing particularly unusual about this fact. CEI focuses on employee issues. The HR department is charged with overseeing employee relations. However, it does suggest that the HR department possesses the influence and corporate presence requisite to successfully drive this kind of initiative. Sometimes this is not the case.

The Human Resources Department Leadership Role

The fact is, although CEI is a critical fundamental (the only one offered in this book that directly speaks to developing an organization's human capital), it is unlikely that senior management will recognize the need for directly addressing it. They assume that the HR department handles such matters. With that said, the HR department has the sole responsibility for getting the ball rolling.

The HR department's management team must provide the vision, direction, and leadership required to get CEI off the ground. Indeed, it should embrace the opportunity to be the architects of the program and volunteer to administer CEI as it takes hold and evolves.

If the HR function currently plays a lesser role in strategic direction-setting within an organization, then it must devise a plan for gaining appropriate access. The key is to take the steps necessary to raise senior management awareness of the need, value, and challenges of the program.

The senior management team must come to better understand the connection between the CEI program and its impact on results. As Figure 9.4 suggests, workforce development provides the foundation for improvements in product and service quality, customer satisfaction, business retention, and, ultimately, growth and profitability.

By demonstrating the program's worth, the HR Department can gain the go-ahead to drive the CEI implementation effort. Once the program gains steam, its administration will surely fall to HR. Once given the formal authority to oversee the program, the department can work to ensure its continued success by maintaining strong communication with senior management—enabling HR to work

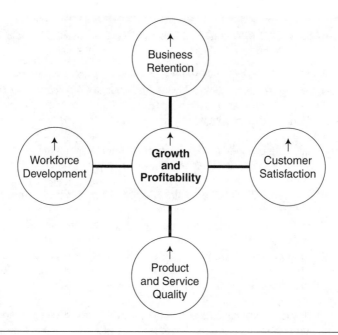

Figure 9.4 Workforce development is the foundation of other bottom-line improvements.

hand-in-hand with the top brass to change the corporate culture associated with employee improvement.

Changing the Performance Measurement Culture

Performance measurement is one of the cultural elements that changes as a result of CEI implementation. Most enterprises already measure and reward performance, but often in inappropriate ways. To gain the most benefit from CEI, organizations should:

- Shift from work measurement to results measurement
- Shift from job descriptions to process descriptions
- Shift from work standards to behavior standards

The process of shifting from work measurement to results measurement forces a concern to take the time to thoughtfully determine, and explicitly define, the outcomes that it seeks. Disciplined thought is required for doing an adequate job of delineating the desired results.

By measuring process outcomes, rather than measuring each step along the way, a different type of measurement framework is established. It is directly tied to business strategy and long-term planning. Adjustments in direction and

---

BEST PRACTICES BUSINESS IN ACTION

A Performance Scorecard at Skanska USA

Skanska USA is a $4 billion construction services company that is located in Parsippany, New Jersey. Its 4100 employees work out of 24 offices throughout the U.S. In an effort to reduce costs and streamline operations, the firm introduced a performance excellence program focused on work measurement and results monitoring.

Initiated in 2003, the program introduced a performance scorecard process to the organization. The scorecard took the corporate vision and business goals and translated them into performance objectives for the employee population. Appropriate measurements were determined for each objective. The measurement criteria, in turn, were folded into an automated management information system that allowed Skanska's 70 senior managers to monitor results and measure outcomes.

Still in place and evolving, the performance scorecard process has helped the enterprise in many ways. For example, it has served to align employee behavior with the company's future vision and goals, placed renewed emphasis on performance and results, and improved the quality and effectiveness of decision-making throughout the concern.

Unquestionably, the effort has functioned to renovate Skanska's corporate culture. Once run as separate and distinct profit centers, the firm's 24 offices are now consolidated and the corporate financials are accurately centralized and managed. Workers are motivated to perform, and management has gained new insights into what is expected and needed to attain results. Skanska USA is a *Best Practices Enterprise™* in the making.

Source: Based on "Skanska USA building: building company drives organizational excellence with scorecard solution," www.microsoft.com, May 9, 2005.

---

strategy require adjustments in performance measurement criteria within such a model. This type of measurement framework helps *Best Practices Enterprises™* keep personnel in lockstep with stratagem (for an example, see Skanska USA sidebar).

Shifting from job descriptions to process descriptions is another necessary step in implementing this new type of performance measurement culture. With the emphasis on outcomes, it is the business processes (not individual job descriptions) that form the basis of measurement within this paradigm. After all, it does not matter whether the shipping specialist does a great job in creating shipping labels if the wrong product is picked from the warehouse. It is the outcome of the process that matters, not the way each job is performed.

Additionally, the move toward process descriptions in defining work duties helps eliminate finger pointing and the "it is not my job" excuses that often come with performance measurement frameworks that demarcate and track individual jobs. Within CEI programs, teamwork and results are what are rewarded. Poor performers are pushed by their teammates to perform, allowing managers to manage the process.

Similarly, this new work culture requires a shift from standardizing work to standardizing worker behavior. If personnel are going to be measured and awarded based on how they perform as a team, then it is in management's best interest to define the behavioral standards that are required by each person.

It is these standards that will be used to supervise individuals as they execute their tasks within business processes. Managers coach staff to help them perform at their best. Company-sponsored training and education are provided to personnel as a means of developing the skills needed for improving organizational performance.

Changing the Training and Education Culture

Training and education are other cultural elements that change as a result of CEI implementation. Most concerns already provide training and education, but seldom in the most effective ways. In fact, many organizations view training and education as a perk, not a requirement for effectiveness, profitability, and growth. To gain the greatest benefit from CEI, organizations should:

- Shift from job training to skills development
- Shift emphasis from operational competences to strategic thinking
- Shift from company-provided to company-sponsored

It is no longer about training personnel to do one job masterfully. In today's quickly changing marketplace, an enterprise must place emphasis on building a well-rounded staff that can provide a broad range of services to the organization. In such environments, training and education are well thought out and specific to what is needed to make the enterprise successful.

CEI stresses teamwork. Personnel are expected to work as a team to get things done.

By shifting from job training to skills development, a firm is making a commitment to prepare staff to think on its feet—better enabling them to do whatever it takes to deliver desired outcomes—even if that means that staff members move beyond the boundaries of their job descriptions to bail out co-workers in need of assistance.

When taken to the next level, an organization would prefer to develop an entire staff that can think beyond their specific area of responsibility. In actual fact, strategic thinking capabilities should be developed within every worker. In this way, businesses can cultivate the best ideas for operational improvement and build the flexibility in thought and action needed for flawless execution.

BEST PRACTICES BUSINESS IN ACTION

The University of Aetna

In an effort to reenergize its sales and service functions, the insurance giant Aetna, Inc. introduced an integrated sales and leadership development program aimed at preparing newly hired college recruits for business in the real world.

The program begins at the Aetna Institute, a company-owned and operated training and development school, where students participate in an intensive 6-week training curriculum highlighted by coursework and role playing. Once the trainees graduate from the classroom, they are shuttled off to field offices for 6 months of on-the-job training and one-on-one coaching. When ready, the recruits begin "play" on their own.

In 2004, the program graduated 22 students. Aetna intends to put 15 to 20 new hires through the program every year. The management team believes that by bringing a diverse group of young professionals in each year (new hires hail from across the country and have earned undergraduate degrees in a wide range of subjects, including art, political science, and anthropology), it is feeding the company's sales and service pipeline for the future.

There is no doubt that with this new recruit training program, Aetna has put an essential element of a CEI program in place. Monitoring how the organization evolves this work in preparation for continued success in the *Best Practices Era* will be interesting.

Source: Based on "Aetna's academy," by Diane Levick, *The Hartford Courant*, August 31, 2004, p. 1E.

Clearly, a shift in emphasis from the development of operational competences to the advancement of strategic thinking capabilities is another cultural change brought about through the institutionalization of CEI.

The shift from company-provided to company-sponsored training and education is another by-product of adopting the CEI framework. Certainly, organizations are responsible for providing training and education to their personnel. However, businesses cannot be the sole source of that training and education.

Staff should seek out additional training to gain the skills that they want to develop on an individualized basis as well. Firms should support and sponsor "extracurricular" education. In this way, the responsibility for employee preparedness is shared by both the employer and the employee, and staff members gain the opportunity to shape their own future at the same time—creating a corporate culture that attracts talent and is highly productive (see the Aetna and Southwest Airlines sidebars for examples).

Marketing of the Corporate Culture

A new and exciting corporate culture emerges as the changes in performance measurement and training and education take hold. The marketing of this

BEST PRACTICES BUSINESS IN ACTION

Enhancing the Employee Experience at Southwest Airlines

Texas-based Southwest Airlines is known for its outstanding customer service and exceptional corporate culture. It is the airline's core belief that happy employees make for happy customers—happy customers become loyal customers.

In an effort to continue to improve its culture, Southwest's reservations department launched a Reservations Agent Job Improvement project aimed at enhancing employee satisfaction. Over 300 staff members were interviewed and special focus groups were formed in order to properly baseline the department's current environment and to establish an action plan to improve job performance and employee gratification.

Several CEI initiatives were identified including:

- New performance review process
- Leadership coaching and mentoring program
- Incentive program redesign project
- Competency and career path modeling project
- Training and learning program

All these efforts are intended to improve productivity and retain high-quality talent. Although the work is still under way, it is apparent that Southwest Airlines is a *Best Practices Enterprise*™ that is focused on remaining competitive through enhancing both the customer and the employee experience.

Source: Based on "LUV is in the air," www.dc.com, 2005.

emerging corporate culture is an essential element of all thriving CEI programs. It helps build and maintain an exceptionally capable and committed workforce.

The marketing message should make clear that the organization is a special place to work in, that it provides ample opportunities to learn and to grow, and that it compensates fairly. The means used to get this message across can include such devices as:

- Recruitment leaflets
- Print advertisements
- Payroll inserts
- Posters/banners
- Orientation packages
- Newsletters/mailings
- Award programs
- Other PR media

In order to gain the most from a marketing effort, content should be crafted to appeal to both internal and external audiences. A two-pronged approach motivates existing staff to perform well and assist in recruitment, while outsiders gain information and perspective on the organization. It is the best way of optimizing related recruitment and retention endeavors and continually fueling the CEI program over time.

Other reminders about what it will take to be successful with CEI follow in the next section.

IN CLOSING

CEI is a multifaceted effort that uses tools such as performance measurement, rewards and incentives, recruiting and retention, and training and education to improve staff performance. Long-term CEI program achievement depends on several factors, including:

- Linking the program to an organization's mission, vision, and values so that CEI becomes an essential cultural element of the concern
- Human resource management stepping up and delivering the "thought leadership" needed to make the CEI effort vital and important to the success of the enterprise
- Allowing the time required to formally plan the CEI implementation effort in order to ensure that the work requisite to continually improve staff is done efficiently and effectively
- Weaving of the CEI continuum into the planning process to make certain that the effort endures

To close, lasting CEI program success is about changing the ways in which management thinks about workers, the ways workers think about work, and the ways in which we motivate them both to change behaviors for the good of the *Best Practices Enterprise*™.

* * *

POSTSCRIPT: FINAL THOUGHTS

*All truly wise thoughts have been thought already thousands of times;
but to make them truly ours, we must think them over again honestly, till
they take root in our personal experience.*
                                        —*Johann Wolfgang von Goethe*

In closing, it is important to note that much of this book focused on shifting organizational culture and adjusting attitudes. It established a vision, defined a set of
iron-clad business principles, and outlined the seven most vital best practices
needed to drive an enterprise to success within the new competitive age of the
early 21st century.

With all that said, let us think about the overarching characteristics that set
The Best Practices Enterprises™ apart from the other organizations with which
they compete. In this way, we establish a *de facto* yardstick with which to measure the overall progress of organizations as they transition forward.

WHAT SETS BEST PRACTICES ENTERPRISES™ APART?

What sets *The Best Practices Enterprises*™ apart from others? Certainly, *Best
Practices Enterprises*™ have all bought into the vision, adopted the principles,
and instituted the seven best practices. But, as a result, they all share six important characteristics that make them "different" from the rest. These characteristics
include:

- Sticking to their strategic vision
- Seeking out bad news

- Adjusting course without hesitation
- Building their corporate cultures deliberately
- Rewarding results
- Imagining the impossible

Let us review each one of these *Best Practices Enterprise*™ characteristics.

Sticking to the Strategic Vision

Best Practices Enterprises™ take care in developing a strategic vision that clearly articulates where the organization will be in the future and how it will get there. Once this vision is defined, time is dedicated to raising awareness of its content among staff and management alike. Yet, unlike other firms that may let the vision collect dust once it is authored, *Best Practices Enterprises*™ stick to their vision. They continuously review and adjust it so that it accurately reflects where the organization is within its business environment. Together with a solid strategic planning program, the strategic vision becomes an important management tool that guides action and informs decision-making within these enterprises—it creates a platform on which best practices thrive.

Seeking Bad News

Best Practices Enterprises™ seek out "bad news." These organizations establish sophisticated feedback mechanisms and communication devices within their communication programs that are needed to bring customer and staff discontent to the surface. In this way, these firms become highly proactive in their actions, while becoming better positioned to anticipate the *needs* and *wants* of their key stakeholders. By refusing to rest on their laurels, these firms remain "hungry"— relentlessly driving toward flawless execution.

Adjusting Course

These organizations are constantly monitoring results and fine-tuning actions in order to remain ahead of the competition. Elegant IT architectures are put into place that can be modified quickly and redeployed as needed in order to support and facilitate midcourse corrections. By choosing to manage strategic initiatives as a portfolio of projects, these firms reduce bureaucracy and build additional flexibility into the work environment. All this serves to help the *Best Practices Enterprise*™ adjust and move on.

Deliberately Building the Culture

Additionally, *Best Practices Enterprises*™ work diligently to build a corporate culture that will support the concern. These organizations are very thoughtful and deliberate about what changes they make and how they make them. They implement the kinds of policies and procedures that reshape the way the workforce thinks and acts. Among other best practices programs, they drive business redesign and workforce inclusion efforts in order to establish a work setting in which commitment and accountability are emphasized and the bar is set high and outstanding performance is expected.

Rewarding Results

With outstanding performance come rewards. These organizations extend traditional performance measurement and reward programs to ensure that their staffs are duly motivated. Their personnel become increasingly satisfied with the work environment because they are regularly challenged, continually recognized, and enthusiastically rewarded. By purposely engaging in *Continuous Employee Improvement* (CEI) activities, *Best Practices Enterprises*™ achieve incredible results.

Imagining the Impossible

Finally, *Best Practices Enterprises*™ regularly spend time imagining the possibilities. They craft and entertain business scenarios that do not exist at the moment, but might possibly occur "down the road." By doing so, these organizations actively anticipate the future. They hedge their bets, avoid marketplace trouble spots, and aggressively pursue opportunities with a nimbleness that other organizations can only dream about.

TIME TO GET GOING

With these characteristics better understood, it is time to set the rest of the strategic agenda outlined in this book into *perpetual* motion. The implementation of these seven best practices is all that is needed to improve performance and ensure lasting success within today's organizations:

- Program-centric strategic planning
- Resilient IT architecture design
- Results-focused communications
- Portfolio-based project management
- Uninterrupted business redesign
- Cross-cultural workforce inclusion
- Continuous employee improvement

Together with the vision and business principles outlined at the outset, the implementation of these practices will help firms flourish within the new business epoch that is upon us.

So, there is no reason to delay—no other methods to consider. In fact, the journey has already begun. Organizations are actively becoming results-focused, customer-responsive, technically resilient, free agent-friendly, cross-cultural, location-independent, and cost-variable. The global marketplace expects nothing less.

Plainly speaking, we are in a time of great business change and renewal. The momentum established thus far is clearly unstoppable. So let us begin to reinvent the rules of global competition in the 21st century; to place focus on the best practices that we know to be essential elements of achieving sustainable world-class performance; and, indeed, to work to realize this exciting new vision of the *Best Practices Enterprise*™.

* * *

SAMPLE CONTINUOUS EMPLOYEE IMPROVEMENT PROJECT BASELINE REPORT

AN INTRODUCTION

In January 2006, XYZ Insurance Corporation (XYZ, resulting from a merger of X Incorporated with YZ Company) embarked upon a continuous employee improvement (CEI) initiative as defined in the program-centric strategic plan for the company. The management team decided to use Kerr Consulting Group's (KCG) proprietary *Strategic Planning Methodology*™ (as depicted in Figure D.1) to drive the strategic planning initiative. The XYZ planning committee recognized that a carefully crafted strategy was important to ensure success in the dynamic global market in which the company competes.

Now, with the new strategic plan in place, it is important to begin implementation of the various *Best Practices* programs identified within it.

The CEI project is one of the first program implementations that the firm has embarked upon. The CEI project team has developed a baseline characterization document that reflects where XYZ is currently in regard to the people, processes, and technology that make up the business. The work delivered in this document will help to inform the training and development and performance measurement elements of the CEI program by defining the strengths and weaknesses of XYZ.

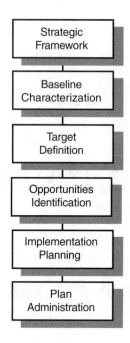

Figure D.1   KCG's *Strategic Planning Methodology*™.

THE METHOD

The team used a workshop approach in developing its baseline characterization. A "workshop prep package" was prepared and distributed to attendees through XYZ's operating committee.

Several baseline workshops were held, including one with the company's planning committee as well as sessions with representatives from each of the major functional areas, including:

- Information systems
- Planning and coordination
- Statistical reporting
- Government affairs
- Human resources
- Claims
- Loss control
- Marketing
- Personal lines
- Claims
- Underwriting
- Financial services

The information gathered in these sessions was then documented and analyzed by the team. The findings were then synthesized into the baseline characterization document.

About the Document

The document is organized along three dimensions:

- People observations
- Process observations
- Technology observations

Additionally, the findings presented within each of the three sections were bundled into various groupings to make the issues uncovered more accessible by XYZ staff.

While there are certainly redundancies among the issues presented in each of the groupings, the CEI project team believes that this taxonomy will make the document easier to reference in the future.

BASELINE ASSESSMENT

What is striking about baseline assessment work is that it usually points to issues that personnel within the organization already know. The XYZ baseline assessment effort proved to be no exception.

However, different may be that issues once thought only to be hunches about the current work environment are now supported by data gleaned from the project team's analysis.

It should be noted that the general assessments presented here reflect what staff members think is *actually* happening within the company's work environment.

The examples presented throughout the document are strictly illustrative. They should not be construed as a "search for the guilty" or a "finger-pointing" exercise.

It is also important to understand that, at times, an individual's sense of reality is shaped by his or her perceptions. The simple fact is that each functional area investigated has significant opportunities for improvement.

In essence, no business area is above scrutiny. What the baseline work has shown is that XYZ has a lot of work to do in order to reach its financial goals by 2010. Here is what was found.

People Observations

The observations provided here relate to the people within the XYZ organization. The observations reflect on those who set policy and direction, those who manage, and all the people who deliver the work product.

As readers explore this section, they should realize that the *people* of XYZ are its real strength. They have endured change at a high rate of speed, they have learned to live in an uncertain world, and yet they have remained loyal and ready to advance.

Leadership issues

- The vision has been defined and employees understand the vision, but they are looking for details about the operational and tactical plans to get there. The implication is that the vision does not mean much if the management team is not willing to do the difficult work needed to make the company successful.
- In many ways, the staff thinks that the current management team does not support them well enough.
- It is widely assumed that the companies were hastily merged together, implying that the expectations placed in the merger effort have been impractical from the start and void of any solid planning. The company seems to be paying the price for its haste as witnessed by its current state of continuous crisis management.
- Leadership, the ability to lead, guide, and delegate, is a critical attribute that senior management must possess for XYZ to be successful. The importance of leadership cannot be overstated.
- Many within the organization view XYZ's leadership as "needing to gel." Decisions take too long, they seem to be motivated by parochial and/or political interests, and they are not clearly communicated. This problem will be mitigated somewhat when the organizational structure is finalized.
- The marketing department is keenly aware that its services are not defined. The department sees a wide array of services that could be delivered, such as marketing research, sales assistance, and communication, but focus must be provided by leadership. For this reason, many in the marketing group feel as if they are "wandering alone in the woods."
- The committee approach to decision making is having a negative impact on the effectiveness of the organization. A senior manager said, "We need a single voice at the top. Companies much larger have a single voice. At XYZ everything is a committee decision."

Managers have the feeling that their "hands are tied" and that they cannot make the business work.

- Many have drawn the conclusion that senior management is driven largely by other interests rather than a business rationale when making decisions.
- Some issues result from a lack of authority rather than a lack of trust. People don't like being told what to do by the new management team.
- Other participants state that they thought there was a lack of trust across departments and that this lack of trust was likely further complicated by the uncertainty of the organization structure and reporting lines.
- Best practices programs of the past have been relative failures and are viewed as a waste of time. For example, the "time management" project was a good idea, but there was little follow-through. High-level support seemed to be lacking.

Uncertainty issues

- Personnel want to have a sense of security in their lives. XYZ staff members are insecure. This organizational uncertainty translates into a myriad of bad behaviors that were often quoted and discussed in the workshops.
- With so many unanswered questions, personnel do not know what to think. Questions seem to permeate the organization: "Do I have a job?" "Who do I report to?" "What will I be doing?" "How much will I be paid?"
- Clearly, *job burnout* has set in. Personnel are beginning to lose interest in making the merger work. There are many reasons for this: long hours, greater workloads, increased demands. Yet, none of these contribute to the burnout more than the uncertainty that exists within the company.
- Complicating matters, there appears to be a lack of corporate identity. Some workshop participants explained, "We need a brand and we need to know what that brand stands for."
- The relationship between the old staff and the new staff complicates matters further. It is believed that much understanding is "lost in the translation"—contributing to a general sense of unease across the company.
- Organizational frustration has resulted from constant changes in corporate direction and decision-making. Former X Incorporated employees become frustrated from the continual change in process,

and former YZ Company employees are generally frustrated by the time it is taking for the two companies to come together.

- There is a great deal of confusion about recent decisions. For example, XYZ made a decision to close down the office automation unit, but left many questions unanswered about how, where, and by whom this work will be performed in the future.
- Fortunately, XYZ has little stratification among the ranks. Senior management remains accessible by all employees. People like this "open door policy."

Communication issues

- The initial decision to announce the merger followed by the seeming inaction has had a negative impact on staff throughout the company. It has allowed rumors to develop. For example, too much time is spent in dismissing such rumors as they spring up among employees.
- Communication is ineffective throughout the company. Formal communications devices such as e-mail, the newsletter, and departmental intranet portals represent steps in the right direction. Yet, these are often misused and do not seem to convey the detailed communications that personnel are seeking.
- There is a feeling that senior management must clearly define and convey the corporate goals and philosophy to the organization.
- It seems that corporate communication, even at department levels, has been put on hold until senior level decisions are finalized. This policy continues to hurt performance within the company.
- Employees are receiving mixed messages. Some employees are allowed paid leave and others are not. Is there favoritism?
- Customers have questions, too. "Who is going to be my underwriter?" "Who do I call if I have problem?" A communication gap clearly exists among stakeholders.
- Interdepartmental communication (among middle management) is also regarded as somewhat deficient. Forums exist in the company for executive management communication and for intradepartmental communication, but effective cross-department communication is lacking.
- Staff members sense that they are receiving incomplete or insufficient information. The recent release of the HR department's *Business Practices Study* was an often-cited example. There is confusion about personnel policies and practices.

Cultural issues

- The different management approaches of the groups have created friction. Many members of one management team are uncomfortable with the management style of the other. Considerable confusion has resulted from communication between the two groups.
- There is some sentiment within XYZ management that some team members do not respect the recommendations of their counterparts. It is also thought that the management team members refuse to define the process through which decisions will be made in the organization. This is seen as time consuming and an expensive way of conducting business.
- The merger has been a catalyst for a culture clash: there are two distinct management cultures and two distinct work planning and execution practices. The differences are widely recognized, yet no plan is in place to address these issues.
- Employees desire autonomy to make decisions and work with the most effective personnel in the company. Many seem to be looking for the nod to go ahead and do what is needed.
- Organizational knowledge also appears to be lacking across the company. Department heads seem to be struggling to understand how all the parts "fit" together.
- XYZ staff members possess a type of "fighting spirit." Personnel think well on their feet and believe in themselves.
- Personnel in the loss control organization think that they are part of a very entrepreneurial organization that has incredibly loyal employees. An attitude of "you can do what you want as long as you do the right thing and it is ethical" is prevalent.
- The lack of headquarter integration perpetuates the perception of two distinctly separate organizations, fueling cultural issues.

Recruitment and retention issues

- Staff members are "burned out." Recruitment and retention of skilled employees are at risk. The economy appears to be acting as an insulator at the moment—keeping staff put. However, turnover is likely when the economy picks up.
- Although recruitment has not been an issue to date, some concern exists that the company's reputation in the market could soon become a problem. People are leaving the firm unhappy.
- Deep impact is felt as a result of experienced individuals, with a deep set of career experiences, leaving the firm.

- In many areas, individual employees represent key knowledge bases that support decision-making or system support. Their retention is considered vital to workflow stability. Cross-training and succession planning may need to be incorporated in management's training.
- Sentiment exists that the company responds very poorly to personnel leaving the firm. Recruiting must hire an experienced resource to replace them, and few documented procedures exist to educate personnel to perform work consistently.
- Finding candidates with the required skill-sets is becoming more difficult, and keeping them is a challenge.
- With all that said, XYZ is viewed as a "nice place to work when stable." This has a positive impact on morale. XYZ is a company that offers flexibility to get the work done and understands the need for a healthy balance between work and family life.

Training issues

- There is no standard for how training is to be delivered. New policies must come out of the CEI effort.
- A comprehensive training program based on standard operating procedures is needed. It will provide many benefits to new hires and experienced staff alike.
- Training needs are plentiful. At every level, there are new ways of doing business and performing work. New training programs are needed to meet these needs.
- Staff members echoed a belief the organization must ensure that time and budgets are allocated to perform needed training activities. Senior management risks its credibility if training is publicly supported, but no resources are allocated to it.
- All staff will require some level of IT training. Yet there is no plan or budget dollars set aside to provide it.

To sum, the issues highlighted above address the people-side of XYZ. The following section looks at the procedural issues facing the company as it continues to normalize post-merger.

Process Observations

The observations provided here relate to the XYZ processes that deliver the products and services to customers of XYZ. Observations regarding product enhancements and marketplace issues are also included in this section.

As readers explore this section, they should pause to recognize that every organization has opportunities to improve the way that it operates. The thoughts and observations reflected in this section of the document point to some of the issues that should be addressed to better position XYZ for continued future success.

Preparedness issues

- It should be noted that the senior management team was often referenced as an impediment to execution. Their apparent inability to gain agreement and work together decisively has contributed to a sense among staff that the company is not prepared to move forward as one.
- An apparent inability to gain agreement and work together decisively clearly indicates that senior management is not prepared to move forward as a team. Work must be done to improve these perceptions or the firm may never be able to garner the employee commitment needed to become what is intended.
- Personnel have the feeling that the "glue" that kept the previous organization's processes working well is now in question. No one knows who to go to for answers and people don't necessarily trust the answers that they receive.
- Throughout the workshops, staff expressed concerns about not feeling prepared to do business as a merged entity. There was a strong sense that there were at least two ways of doing things (X-style and Y-style, reflecting the two management approaches). The fact is, one way should be defined, documented, and trained or mistakes will continue to be made.

Process improvement issues

- Business process improvement work will be needed this year to streamline all operations across XYZ.
- A process to formalize the process of establishing service commitments to new clients and brokers is also being adopted. The success of this process improvement will hinge on redefining the relationship among departments.
- A "service center" approach, for example, is planned for implementation. This approach will centralize the processing of high-frequency, low-exposure transactions within the organization. Customers can access the center through a kiosk to adjust their account information.
- Many departments are going through a redefinition process. Each must fully understand the best method for delivering service and value to the company.
- Many departments are finding it difficult to define service standards and market strategies in the current merger-focused environment.

- The process of redefining the business processes across operations should be recognized as important initiatives as well.
- On the brighter side, XYZ is effectively using temporary talent to address capacity and talent gaps.

Procedures and documentation issues

- It is true that policies and procedures had existed in various forms throughout the former X and YZ organizations. It seems that many were not documented or were simply "hearsay." Consequently, the quality, style, and perceived value of many of the existing policies and procedures have become somewhat lost as the company works through merger issues. It seems that the links to the traditions of the past are becoming broken as former X and YZ reporting lines blur.
- Not surprisingly, many departments want to go back to the "way it's always been done." The result is that procedures are performed differently by geographic location and by manager—contributing to error and confusion across the company.
- However, some bright light exists. Members of the underwriting department are very proud of the effectiveness of existing policies and procedures in their group. One employee made the comment: "Our policies and procedures are recognized as some of the best in the industry." Their written procedures have allowed the organization to effectively merge and operate efficiently within the current environment.
- Clearly, new CEI procedures will benefit the company in areas such as new hire training, interdepartmental communication, and standardized processing across locations. A standard set of CEI policies and procedures should be developed and institutionalized.

Management information issues

- The financial services department, in particular, is impacted by the differing financial approaches of the former YZ and X operations. In many ways, financial services cannot fully move forward with a financial reporting method until key decisions are made on this subject.
- Furthermore, it appears that too few individuals are sufficiently trained on the management reporting tools. A backlog of reporting requirements exists.
- It has also been noted that XYZ will need the ability to "slice and dice" its information in different ways in order to meet senior management's needs.

- Many XYZ staff members think that management information systems (MISs) are inadequate. More effort needs to be put toward producing decision-making information for use by managers across the company. To accomplish this, key philosophical differences must be remedied.

Market and profitability issues

- On a positive note, the staff members in personal lines have demonstrated loyalty and dedication throughout the years. This area represents a possible growth opportunity for the company.
- Otherwise, market conditions exist that could be a real threat to the XYZ's business environment. The industry is moving from a "hard" market into a "softer" one, putting pressure on pricing.
- The competition is changing and adjusting. For instance, ABC Insurance has made great efforts to outsource and streamline operations—making them a difficult opponent to overcome. IMR Corporation, on the other hand, appears to be in a weakened state because of recent exposures and poor customer service. XYZ could exploit such weaknesses through deliberate effort.
- New terrorism coverage requirements put additional pressure on the company. It is contributing to diminishing bottom-line improvements.
- The market in which XYZ competes presents many challenges and opportunities. One thought is that XYZ can leverage the size of its parent, but XYZ must first address some of the challenges that exist within the newly merged company.

Technology Observations

The observations provided here relate to the information systems technologies supporting the XYZ work activities. When reading this section, the reader is cautioned to recognize that the IT work effort is generally recognized positively. However, there are many unresolved issues (presented below) that must be addressed.

Application system issues

- The fragmentation of XYZ systems results in an unproductive work environment in many areas such as underwriting and financial reporting. Additionally, existing limitations prevent personnel from readily extracting necessary data.
- System limitations may continue to perpetuate the separation of cultures because important data needed for decision-making still exist within individual remote workstations.

- System and data integration is vital to XYZ. Too many islands of information exist within the company. To become a more effective organization, XYZ must reduce the use of multiple applications, individual databases, and technology platforms.
- The reliability of systems is being called into question. A feeling exists that migrating this new data into the systems will create increased instability and data issues.
- The general impression from the business units is that applications and network resources crash too often. This has a measurable economic impact on the business in lost productivity and decreased service.
- The Claims Entry System is considered to be a generally dependable system in the XYZ environment, although it is quickly becoming obsolete.
- The Risk Manager System is viewed favorably by its users within the company. As long as it is enhanced appropriately, the system is looked at as a reliable and stable system that will support the needs of the immediate future.
- There is recognition that the technology environment has come a long way in the past year. Yet, a sense remains that the technology environment must achieve greater improvement to effectively support the business in the long term.
- The commercial lines operation also has systems needs. The implementation of a solution to their system deficits (such as that available in the Applied Agency Management System) is a glaring need, as is phone system infrastructure support.
- Like many other business units, the financial services group is also a victim of fragmented IT systems. The financial services group is impacted by the large multiplicity of systems in the organization and confusion over appropriate source systems needed for accurate management reporting.
- The Claims File System is looked at as a key strength for the claims department. It has delivered the necessary functionality on a flexible platform for distribution to the various branches.
- A key initiative for the claims department is to provide a connection between the existing Rookie System and the Claims File System. This will provide an ability to track, from a holistic sense, the claims being processed by the organization.

IT support issues

- Many in the business are confused by how IT is structured. There is considerable confusion about who to call or who is responsible for different applications or systems.
- The management team within the IT department is keenly aware of the challenges of the next several years. They are proactively seeking ways of improving internal customer service.
- The help desk appears to be timely and responsive. An issue may exist when urgent ("deadline driven") tasks are routed directly to developers (i.e., circumventing the help desk process).
- Remote access (via VPN) to technology resources in the company does not provide the ability for employees to perform their work outside the office.
- The customer support unit is processing many of its transactions via manual procedures. Customers often get information before the XYZ staff, which threatens the credibility of the operation.
- Demands for data from external customers and vendors are increasing. These entities are requesting data that present systems do not capture or process effectively.
- It has been noted that the new IT organization has not supported the Loss Manager product properly since the beginning of the year. Because customers are demanding more access to information, the loss control department is investigating a web-based version of this system.
- The loss control department has experienced a very high level of frustration with the level of support from the IT department. Connecting to the network through a VPN and the promised modifications to the Notes environment that were not delivered are a source of this frustration.
- IT principles are being adopted that redefine how IT services are delivered throughout the company. Industry best practice models are being incorporated into the work product. Once published and presented to business management, this work could help with improving the IT department's public relations within the user community.

Vendor reliance issues

- Besides the obvious IT vendor relationships, there are subtle relationships forming, as well. Outsourcing continues to be discussed, for example. These new relationships must be nurtured.
- XYZ is heavily reliant on outside vendors for providing services for system development and ongoing support. This reliance may create a

significant threat if vendors shift directions or if they evolve away from providing services required by XYZ. Prudent vendor management policies need to be implemented.

- New hires to this department will need additional training that is specific to the company. Otherwise, key knowledge may be lost if turnover occurs.
- As the company continues to move away from reliance on internal assets, it must ensure that the technologies intended to replace those services are up to par.

The issues presented above highlight the underpinnings of the company's technology challenges. The intent is that work needed to address the challenges will translate into project/program initiatives that will be staffed and funded in the near future.

IN CLOSING

Although there may be no major revelations here, the work needed to overcome the issues may be seen as quite intimidating by many within XYZ. Keep in mind, X Company has just merged with YZ and many of these issues are to be expected. With that said, management and staff alike should view these findings as an important call to arms and view the CEI program as an important element of future success.

The CEI project represents an opportunity to address in an informal and focused way the various people, process, and technology issues uncovered. New and exciting training and development and performance measurement elements can be folded into the company to exploit strengths and overcome weaknesses. In this way, XYZ can become a recognized *Best Practices Enterprise*™ of the future.

* * *

INDEX

A

Achieve Healthcare Technologies, 112
Adjusting course, 194
Aerospace, 37
Aetna Institute, 190
Allied Domecq, 62
Alternative scenarios, 44
Annual budget planning, 19, 32, 142
A.T. Kearney, 37
Audi AG, 178
Automation
    competition and, 9
    for METRO Group, 8
    process redefinition prior to, 125
    robust, easily modifiable, 75–76
    tools, 90
Automotive/engine industry
    Audi AG, 178
    BMW, 125, 126
    Cummins, 126, 127
    DaimlerChrysler, 185
    Ford Motor Company, 146, 147, 166, 167
    Rolls-Royce Aerospace, 36, 37
Autonomy, 22

B

Bad news, 194
Bangkok Bank, 134

BAT Group (British American Tobacco, plc), 9
Belgian Telecom Company, 120, 121
Best-of-breed vendors, 24–25
Best practices business principles
    fitting together, 11, 12, 14, 32, 60, 106, 124, 142, 160, 176
    list of fifteen, 14–15
    new era, new agenda, 13–15
    principle 1, 15–16
    principle 2, 16–17
    principle 3, 18
    principle 4, 19
    principle 5, 19–20
    principle 6, 20–21
    principle 7, 21–22
    principle 8, 22–23
    principle 9, 23
    principle 10, 24
    principle 11, 24–25
    principle 12, 25–26
    principle 13, 26–27
    principle 14, 27–28
    principle 15, 28
    seven business programs, 195–196
Best Practices Enterprise, 1–12, 124
    characteristics shared, 193–194
    new vision, new era, 1–12
    philosophy, 10–12

seven business programs
constituting, 11–12, 195–196
Best Practices Era, 63, 122, 124, 125
Best Practices World, 73
BMW (Bimmer), 125, 126
Bowne & Co., 63
BP (British Petroleum), 166, 168
Brain trust, 120
Brand Solutions, LLC, 4
Breakthrough improvement
opportunities, 130
British American Tobacco, plc
(BAT Group), 9
Bureaucracy, 10, 28
Business modeling, 129–130
Business principles. *See* Best
practices business principles
Business process redesign (BPR)
initiative, 73, 135
Business variability. *See* Variable
business enterprise

C

Call center, India, 160
Campus area networks. *See* CANs
CANs (campus area networks),
90–91
CDO (chief diversity officer), 169,
171
diversity administration, 167, 168,
169
diversity and inclusion charter,
170
diversity framework strategy, 164
diversity-in-action recognition
programs, 170
launch of project, 162–162
maintaining program momentum,
169–170
new behavior paradigm, 163–164

CEI (continuous employee
improvement), 26–27,
175–192. *See also XYZ
Insurance Corporation*
baseline evaluation, 179
competitive analysis, 180–181
continuum, 177–179
corporate culture, marketing of,
190–192
driving the program, 186–192
human resources' leadership role,
186–187
opportunity identification
template, 56–57
performance measurement, 181,
182, 187–189
program development, 180–186
recruitment practices, 183
retention practices, 184
reward and incentive packages,
181–183
skills assessment, 180
strategy planning, 179–186
training and education culture,
189–190
training practices, 184–186
CEO (chief executive officer)
in cross-cultural workforce
inclusion, 162
diversity administration and, 168
executive steering committee and,
111–112
CFO (chief financial officer), 32
Chain of command, 16–17, 28
Chief diversity officer. *See* CDO
Chief executive officer. *See* CEO
Chief financial officer. *See* CFO
Chief planning officer. *See* CPO
City of San Diego, 7
Claim assignment, 138

Client-server implementation types, 101
COGs (conceptual operations groups)
  in case study, 137–139
  in event model, 138
  loss reporting, 137–138
  operations view, 79–80, 82
  in value chains, 131–133, 137–139
  work units and, 92–93
Color blindness, 23, 173
Commercial Electronic Office Business Portal (CEO Portal), 70
Common language and procedures, 120, 121
Communication. *See also* Results-focused communications
  comprehensive program, 9–10, 24
  cross-agency task force, 144
  devices, 50–51
  infrastructure, 121
  issues, CEI project baseline report, 202
  in portfolio-based project management, 108, 117
  procedures and documentation, 206
  in RITA administration, 75
  vehicles, 147–154
Competitive analysis, 180–181
Comptroller, 32
Computing
  Internet, 31
  networked, 88–92
Conceptual operations groups. *See* COGs
Consultant, 163. *See also* Free agent
Continual transformation, 15–16, 124
Continuous employee improvement, *See* CEI

Continuous process improvement, 72, 74
Continuous transformation, 15–16, 124
Contract administration, 26
Coors Brewing Company, 74, 75
Corporate bureaucracy, 10
Corporate culture. *See also* Diversity and inclusion
  building deliberately, 194–195
  change, project management and, 108
  chic, 161
  issues, CEI project baseline report, 203
  marketing of, 190–192
  project culture orientation, 113
CPO (chief planning officer), 42, 112
Cross-cultural workforce inclusion, 159–174
  business case, defining, 161–162
  CEO sponsorship, 162
Cross-project coordination procedure, 116
Culture. *See* Corporate culture
Cummins, 126, 127
Customization, 4, 125, 126

D
DaimlerChrysler, 185
Data management tools, 71
Deakin, Emily, 168
Deliverables, 66, 92
Demings, W. Edwards, 148
Department of Homeland Security, 157
Department of Revenue Services. *See* DRS
Direct marketing, 126
Distributed point-of-sale (POS) system, 62

Diversity and inclusion, 10, 23, 173.
See also Cross-cultural
workforce inclusion
Documentation and procedures, 206
DRS (Department of Revenue
Services), 144
Dunkin' Brands, Inc., 62

E
E-bulletin board, 151
ECD (Executive Council on Diversity
and Work Life), 167
E-commerce, 71
EDI (electronic data interchange), 91
EDS (Electronic Data Systems), 37,
74
EEOC (Equal Employment
Opportunity Commission),
171, 172
EEO initiative, 55
EIS (executive information systems)
applications, 151, 152, 153
Electronic data interchange. *See* EDI
Electronic Data Systems. *See* EDS
E-mail, 90, 155
Employee. *See also* Continuous
employee improvement;
Cross-cultural workforce
inclusion; Reward and
incentive practices
burnout, 171–172, 201, 203
differences, 163
morale, 143
recognition, 170
recruitment practices, 183,
203–204
resource groups (ERGs), 167
retention practices, 184, 203–204
satisfaction, 191
turnover, 160
Enron, 156

Entrepreneur. *See Your Company, Inc.*
Equal Employment Opportunity
Commission. *See* EEOC
ERGs (employee resource groups),
167
Error recording, 3
ESC (executive steering committee)
formation of, 39–40
in portfolio-based project
management, 110, 111–112
in program-centric strategic
planning, 35
trouble with, 43
Eskom, 175, 176
Ethnocentricity, 171
Event model excerpt, 138
Executive Council on Diversity and
Work Life. *See* ECD
Executive information systems.
See EIS
Executive management. *See also*
CEO; Strategic planning office
(SPO)
administration process and, 76
business principles and, 15
executive steering committee,
110, 111–112
for portfolio-based PM, 116
in portfolio-based PM, 121
preparedness issues, 205
Executive steering committee. *See*
ESC

F
Fast-food IT architecture, 62
Federal government, 72, 157
File transfer, 91
FNAC, 2
Ford Communications Network, 146

Ford Motor Company, 146, 147, 166,
167
Fortune 500 firm, 35
Foundation-setting, 108
Free agent. *See also Your Company,
Inc.*
in city of San Diego, 7
market, leveraging of, 22–23
portfolio-based PM and, 106
FutureScape team, 39

G

GAE (generic application
environments), 88
Gap analysis, 71
Gender neutrality, 23, 173
Generic application environments.
See GAE
Geographical boundaries. *See*
Physical boundaries for
business processess
German chemical company, 45
Germany, 8, 45, 178
Global integration, 126
Globalization of business, 143
Global marketplace, 161, 174
Graphical user interface. *See* GUI
GUI (graphical user interface), 138

H

Hammer, Michael, 123
Hartford, The, 152
Hartness International, 3
Healthcare industry, 106, 113
Achieve Healthcare
Technologies, 112
Johns Hopkins Hospital, 148,
149
St. Peter's Hospital, 106, 107
TeleDoc 5000 system, 5
Wellpoint, 130, 131

HERO (Hartness Error Recording
Online), 3
Hierarchy of departments, 20
Hiring. *See* Free agent; Human
resources
Hoechst AG, 45
HP Indigo Press 3000, 126
Human capital study, 176
Human resources, 113, 176, 186–187.
See also CEI

I

Imagining the impossible, 195
Inclusion. *See* Cross-cultural
workforce inclusion; Diversity
and inclusion
Independent contractor. *See* Free
agent
India, 160
call center, 160
Industry standard technnology tool
suites, 9
Information systems architecture.
See ISA
Information technology. *See* IT
Insurance value chain case study,
137–139
Intercompany relationships, 25–26
International Survey Research, 142
Internet, 3, 31, 107
ISA (information systems
architecture), 62
IT architecture. *See* Resilient IT
architecture design program
IT architecture analogy, 61
IT environment
architecture, 21–22
baseline characterization, 64, 65
on-demand infrastructure, 74
questions, three simple, 63, 64
support issues, 209

J

Jewelers Mutual (JM) Insurance
Company, 116, 117
Johns Hopkins Hospital, 148, 149

K

Kerr Consulting Group, 103
Kraft Foods, 166

L

Labor force. *See* Continuous
employee improvement
program; Free agent
LANs (local area networks), 90, 91
Leadership, 200–201
Leakage, health claims, 131
Local area networks. *See* LANs

M

Management bureaucracy, 28
Management information issues,
206–207
Marine Corps, 73, 75
Market and profitability, 207
Marketing, 126
Marsh & McLennan, 156
Mass customization, 4, 125
MCI, 156
Merrill Lynch, 6
METRO Group, 8
Mission statements, 28, 44
Mobile computing, 90
Multiple workgroup processors, 91

N

NEC's TeleDoc 5000 system, 5
Nestlé USA, 124, 125
Network computing. *See also* Target
definition document
connectivity tiers, 90–91
LAN workstation connectivity, 91
templates for, 91–92

three levels of, 88–90
New markets, 161
9/11, 156, 157
Normalized work model, 79

O

ODI (Office of Diversity and
Inclusion), 169–170
opportunity identification
template, 54–55
program establishment, 162–169
program measurement accord, 165
roadblocks, 171–172
success in diversity game,
172–174
team formation, 163
training and promotion, 165–166
Office of Diversity and Inclusion.
See ODI
On-demand IT infrastructure, 74
Online shift bidding, 107
Opportunities identification
documents, 47–57
continuous employee improvement
program, 56–57
cross-cultural workforce inclusion
program, 54–55
portfolio-based project management
program, 52–53, 115–116
program-centric strategic
planning, 48–49
resilient IT architecture (RITA)
design program, 49–50
results-focused communication
program, 50–51
uninterrupted business redesign
program (U-BPR), 53–54
Opportunity planning template.
See Opportunities
identification documents
Organizational knowledge, 7

Organizational memory, 19
Outside assistance, 121. *See also*
    Free agent
Outsourcing, 5, 24–25

P

Padgett-Thompson, 114
People issues, 138
PeopleSoft's Payroll and Human
    Capital Management software,
    185
Performance measurement
    in CEI program, 56–57, 181
    culture changing and, 187–189
    results orientation of, 27–28
Performance scorecard, 188
Physical boundaries for business
    processes, 17, 18
Physical plant, 18
Physician, telemedicine, 5
Pie charts, best practices, 11, 14, 32,
    60, 106, 124, 142, 160, 176
Pinaul-Printemps-Redoute Group, 2
Planning horizons, 72
Plateaus, 71–72
PM (project management), 52,
    110–111
PM Boot Camp, 113, 114
PMO (project management office),
    75
Point-of-sale (POS) system, 62
Portfolio-based project management
    program, 105–121
    common hazards, 118–119
    critical success factors, 119–121
    free agency and, 106
    obstacles to consider, 107–109
    opportunity identification
        template, 52–53
    portfolio management and
        administration, 116–118

project identification and priority
    setting, 115–116
project roles and responsibilities
    awareness program, 110–112
project skills development,
    113–115
rationale and implications, 20–21
structure, 109–118
Price Waterhouse Coopers, 120
Procedures and documentation, 206
Process analysis, 130
Process improvement, 205–206
Profitability and market, 207
Program-centric strategic planning,
    31–45
    benefits of, 36
    charging the team, 38–39
    establishing project, 38
    executive steering committee
        formation, 39–40
    explained, 32–33
    getting started, 37–42
    initiative types in, 33
    opportunity identification
        template, 48–49
    perfect program, 34–37
    planning process, 40–41
    project planning training, 42
    provisions characterizing, 34–35
    staying current, 33–34
    strategic planning office, 41–42,
        43
Project-based skills
    bottom-up project management,
        114–115
    deficits, 109
    development, 113–115
    top-down project management,
        113–114
Project champion, 38
Project management. *See* PM

Project management office. *See* PMO
Project opportunities template. *See* opportunities identification documents
Project skills. *See* Skills
Project sponsor, 110, 111
Project team, 110, 111

Q
Quality reviews, 148

R
Race Summit, 168
Radio frequency identification. *See* RFID
Recruitment practices, 183, 203–204
Redi-Mail, 126
Reference services, 87
Remote work locations, 18
Resilient IT architecture design program. *See* RITA
Responsiveness, 126
Results-focused communications, 141–157. *See also* Communication
  baseline establishment, 145, 146
  executive information systems, 151
  initiation of, 145–147
  intranet bulletin boards, 149, 151
  "lessons learned" chronicle, 148–149, 150
  newsletters, 153–154
  opportunity identification template, 50–51
  pointers for success, 154–157
  program, intentions of, 143–144
  project coordination meetings, 154
  project formation, 145
  quality reviews, 148, 150
  road shows, 152, 153

stakeholder assessment, 145
status reports, 148
target environment definition, 146–147
vehicles for communication, 147–154
Retention practices, 184, 203–204
Reward and incentive practices, 181–183, 195
RFID (radio frequency identification) technology, 8
RITA (resilient IT architecture design program), 59–76. *See also* RITA six-step approach; Target definition document; Target template
  applications view, 85–86, 87–88
  basic dimensions, 64–66
  building construction analogy, 61, 78
  built-in resilience, 62–63
  essence of architectures, 61–64
  explained, 60–61
  information view, 82–85
  methodology, 64–66
  operations view, 79–82
  opportunity identification template, 49–50
  single system view as goal, 86–87
  six-step approach, 66–75
  technology view, 88–92
  three-pronged approach, 75
  views of, 78
RITA administration, 74–75
RITA framework, 66–68
  target definition, 69–71
RITA six-step approach
  baseline characterization, 68–69
  implementation planning, 71–73
  opportunities identification, 71
Rolls-Royce Aerospace, 36, 37

Routine activities. *See* Outsourcing

S

SAFECOM, 156, 157
Sample opportunities identification
    documents. *See* ODI
San Diego, City of, 7
Sarbanes-Oxley regulations, 33, 156
Scope creep, 148
Self-employment, 22. *See also* Free
    agent
Self-sustaining organization, 25
Senior management. *See* Executive
    management
September 11, 2001, 156, 157
Service delivery, 4, 125
Shared mental models, 27
Shaw, Gordon, 45
Siemens Nixdorf Information
    Systems. *See* SNI
Silo mentality, 17
Six Sigma Statistical Analysis, 127
Skanska USA, 188
Skills, 113. *See also* Project-based
    skills
SME (subject matter expert), 110,
    111
SNI (Siemens Nixdorf Information
    Systems), 39
Social responsibility, 161
Software, 185
Southwest Airlines, 190, 191
SPO (strategic planning office)
    formation, 41
    nurturing, 120–121
    for portfolio-based PM, 110, 112,
        116–117
    positioning within
        organization, 42
    trouble on high, 43
Sponsor review meetings (SRMs), 73

Standard opportunity identification
    template. *See* Opportunities
    identification documents
Statement of Requirements (SoR),
    157
State of the union, 143, 144
Store-in-a-Box, FNAC strategy, 2
St. Peter's Hospital, 106, 107
Strategic planning. *See also* Program-
    centric strategic planning
    completion of initiatives, 19–20
    as continuously performed
        process, 8, 19
    program-centric, 109, 121
Strategic planning office. *See* SPO
Strategic vision. *See* Vision
Subject matter expert. *See* SME

T

Takeout Taxi, 4
Target definition document. *See also*
    Template
    applications view, 85–86, 87–88
    four views of RITA, 78–86, 88–92
    information view, 82–85
    integration opportunity, 92, 95,
        96, 97
    operations view, 79–82
    single system view as goal, 86–87
    target architecture, 77–78
    target templates, 92–103
    technology view, 88–92
Target template
    application characteristics, 93, 95
    application to GAE affinity
        matrix, 99, 100
    characteristics of information, 97,
        100
    COG to current organization
        matrix, 93–94

COGs to user class affinity
matrix, 93, 94
data groups to level of computing,
102, 103
integration opportunity, 95, 96, 97
target application access by
physical location, 97, 98
target application to client/server
implementation type, 99, 101
target application to data grouping
affinity, 93, 94
target application to existing
application, 95, 97
target application to level of
computing, 99, 102
target application to target
application, 95, 96
target application to user class,
95, 97, 98
target COGs to data grouping, 97,
99
target COGs to target application,
95, 96
Tax department, 144
Team, 111
Team-based management model, 28
Teamwork
for inclusion, 163
project room, 128
training, 113
Technology. *See also* Network
computing
application systems issues,
207–208
issues, value chain case study, 139
Telecommuting, 6
TeleDoc 5000 system, 5
TELUS, 153
Template. *See* Target template
Temporary worker. *See* Free agent
Terrorism, 156

Think out of the box, 133
3M's planning story, 44, 45
Training and education
in CEI programs, 10, 56–57,
184–186
culture, changing, 189–190
for diversity, 165–170
insufficient, 172
issues, CEI project baseline
report, 204
on-demand, 185
training department, 113
Transition planning, 133
24/7 Customer, 160

U
U-BPR. *See* Uninterrupted business
redesign program
Ultra-responsiveness, 126
Uncertainty issues, 201–202
Uninterrupted business redesign
program (U-BPR), 123–136
BPR project review, 135
business modeling, 129–130
instituting the philosophy,
134–135
keys to, 126–134
ongoing basis for, 17
opportunity identification
template, 53–54
process analysis, 130
reasons to embrace, 124–126
setting, establishment of, 128
team building, 127–128
transition planning, 133
value chain, 130–133
United States Marine Corps (USMC),
72, 73, 75
Unsurpassed service delivery, 4, 125
Urgent news communications
strategies, 156

U.S. Department of Homeland
   Security, 157
U.S. Government, 72

V
Value added network (VAN), 91
Value chain. *See also* Target template
   case study, 137–139
   COGs, defining, 137
   diagram, sample, 132–133
   five distinct components, 79,
      132–133
   loss reporting, 137–138
   performance element, 81
   planning element, 80
   staffing element, 80–81
   support element, 81–82
   training element, 81
   for U-BPR, 130–133
"Variable" business enterprise, 6,
   24–25
Vendor contracting relationships,
   25–26
Vendor reliance issues, 209–210
Virtual market, 6
Vision
   establishment of, 193, 196
   mission and, 28
   new, for new era, 1–12
   quotation, 1
   sticking to, 194
   strategic plan and, 34, 44

W
War room, 128
Wellpoint, 130, 131
Wells Fargo & Co., 70

Wide area networks (WANs), 91
Workflow, 129
Workflow fluidity, 3
Workflow organization and design,
   125
Workforce. *See* Employee
Workforce diversity, 10
Workgroup servers, 91
Work-in-process (WIP) application,
   86–87

X
XYZ Insurance Corporation. *See also*
   Target template
   applications view, 85–86, 87–88
   baseline assessment, CEI report,
      199–210
   CEI project baseline report,
      197–210
   information view, 82–85
   introduction, CEI report, 197–198
   IT environment at, 78–91
   method, CEI report, 198–199
   operations view, 79–82
   people observations, CEI report,
      200–204
   process observations, CEI report,
      204–207
   single system view as goal, 86–87
   target views, 78–79
   technology observations, CEI
      report, 207–210
   technology view, 88–92

Y
Your Company, Inc., 2–10